SIMPLY WONDERWOMAN

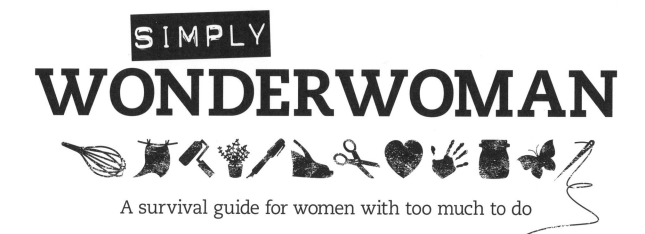

A survival guide for women with too much to do

Joanna Gosling

Photography by Rachel Whiting

KYLE BOOKS

For Craig, Maya, Iona and Honor

First published in Great Britain in 2011 by
Kyle Books
23 Howland Street
London, W1T 4AY
general.enquiries@kylebooks.com
www.kylebooks.com

ISBN: 978-0-85783-058-6

Editor: Catharine Robertson
Designer: Laura Woussen
Photographer: Rachel Whiting
Photographer's assistant: Rita Platts
Stylist: Victoria Fitchett
Copy editor: Sally MacEachern
Production: David Hearn and Nic Jones

A Cataloguing In Publication record for this title is available from the British Library.

Colour reproduction by Alta Image
Printed and bound in China by Toppan Leefung Printing Ltd.

SIMPLY
WONDERWOMAN

CONTENTS

LIKE ANY WORKING MOTHER, I KNOW WHAT IT'S LIKE TO HAVE TOO MUCH TO DO AND NOT ENOUGH TIME TO CRAM IT ALL IN. NO TIME TO STOP AND THINK. THE PRESSURE OF FEELING LIKE YOU'RE ALWAYS FAILING ON AT LEAST ONE FRONT.

The problem is we covet an impossible ideal, as we eye the image of the baking, homemaking, perfect wife and mother, on top of working (whether out of choice or necessity), and the basic unavoidable day-to-day running of a home. Inevitably, trying to be everything can leave us feeling like the wheels are about to come flying off all the time. We want to be Wonderwoman, but the reality is no-one can really embody everything that we imagine her to be.

So we need to think smart. Simplify and streamline our lives where we can, so we free up headspace and time to spend on the nice things that keep us sane.

Simply Wonderwoman's mantra is 'minimum effort, maximum return.' I love the eureka moment of discovering a great corner-cutting method or tip that really works. I'm compulsive about gathering them from friends, family and people I meet. For instance, I got a brilliant sewing tip from a director at work, who was watching me trying in vain to thread a needle (don't ask me why I was sewing in the studio!). I even got a great cat tip from a rock star I happened to be interviewing on the day we were going to collect our new pet.

Everyone has a great tip to pass on. Obviously I've picked up a lot from my mother and grandmother – the models of domesticity I grew up with. And I love stumbling upon things myself that work so brilliantly I instantly want to call everyone I know and tell them about it. So there are time-saving, money-saving and job-avoidance tips galore in the book.

But life is not about running a home brilliantly, although doing it is the means to an end. Think of your home as being like a business – once the systems and strategies are set up, things get a whole lot easier. If you can get the day-to-to-day machinery of life to work as smoothly as possible, it frees you up to do the nice stuff. The stuff that relaxes you and makes you feel satisfied, so you don't keep coming to the end of another crazy day thinking, 'Is that really what it's about?'

Which brings us to the image of the perfect homemaker. It's appealing because creating something – doing something you don't actually have to do – is satisfying. Baking a cake, for instance, gives pleasure because while you are making it, other thoughts and worries go out of your head as you focus on the creative process. It actually clears headspace. And then giving the cake to others to enjoy brings you so much more pleasure than if you had just gone out and bought one. So, the book is divided into two halves. The first covers the basics; the second covers the nice stuff. In the second part, the mantra becomes 'the return is worth the investment'. But it is still about keeping everything simple. If I look at a recipe and it has a really long list of ingredients, I automatically think it's too much hassle, and will look elsewhere for a simpler version. It's the same with everything I make and do – keep it simple. So, this is about creating really lovely things to make your home a nicer place, or to give to others, with very little time and effort and zero skill.

The final mantra is 'do one thing each day'. We're trying to simplify and streamline here, not continue with the overloading. So the book is laid out in bite-sized chunks, with the idea being that you can pick out one thing each day that really is worth doing, to change your life for the better.

PART ONE
THE BASICS

THIS IS ABOUT HOW TO GET STUFF DONE – the business of running a home – in the easiest and quickest way. Minimum effort, maximum return. It's not about sweeping the dust under the carpet. Not doing the chores – tempting as it sounds – is counterproductive because a messy, dirty, chaotic house impacts on your well-being and ability to think clearly. This is about getting things done fast and efficiently, with effective corner-cutting.

It's about getting your life organised, so you avert panics and disasters that can make the wheels come off. It's about helping you to be in control. Think of time as currency. This section is about how to save it, so you can spend it doing something you actually want to do – making time for friends and family, taking a cookery class or a dance lesson, or making something. And don't forget to just 'do one thing each day'. It's always best to build in small increments (break everything down) little and often. Don't plunge right in and go crazy trying to do everything all at once – that's the fastest route to a nervous breakdown. Know when you're at your limits. Stop, pull back, and do something nice. Sometimes when life is getting on top of you, a little time out – just taking a bath with a cup of tea and a good book or a magazine, or going out for a walk – is enough to rebalance you.

Getting
ORGANISED

I WROTE THIS BOOK because for too long I had felt

I was skimming along, just about keeping the balls in the

air, but perilously close to letting them fall. It was

like my head was full. I had no space or time to think.

It took me far too long to work out that the best

way to clear some headspace was to get organised.

First Things First

START THE DAY WITH A LIST OF THREE

There's nothing new in writing a to-do list, but it's still the best way to declutter your mind and avoid that horrible rising panic when you feel like you've got too much to do and not enough time to do it. The trick with a to-do list is to keep it simple. Get in the habit of starting the day by drawing up a list of a maximum of three things that must get done. Be realistic. If there's something time-consuming that you keep putting off, make it the only thing on your list. When a to-do list is too long, it's counterproductive because it just makes your heart sink every time you look at it, and are reminded of how much you have to do. Remember, it's better to achieve just one thing each day that you have prioritised, rather than stick seven things down that leave your head swimming and that you probably won't get done. If something's not done on the day you put it on the list, chances are it won't be any time soon because the sense of urgency is gone. Little and often gets things done calmly and effectively.

KEEP A DIARY, NOTEBOOK AND PEN IN YOUR BAG

One year I decided it would be a fabulously stylish idea to have a nice large desk diary rather than a little one in my bag. What a disaster. I never remembered to write anything down and was constantly forgetting what I'd planned. Basically it made me realise that if I don't write something down instantly, I will forget it. Or remember it at the wrong time. So now my number one golden rule about being organised is really the most obvious one of all – make a note of everything the instant you think of it or arrange it. To this end I keep my diary with me at all times. Honestly, it's good for peace of mind, apart from anything. I spent a whole year worrying I had early onset dementia. There's just too much you're trying to cram in to your brain when you're juggling work and motherhood, so take the pressure off by taking a second to make a note of your plans. Keep a notebook in your bag too, for writing down shopping lists, ideas, a tip you've just picked up – anything and everything as you think of it.

Put up a door peg

This is a simple but utterly foolproof way of making
sure you never forget anything when you leave the
house – a clothes peg stuck to the door. Things are
literally there right in front of you as you leave, so you
simply can't forget. The shopping list, school activity
reply slip, letter to post, a cheque you need to pay into
the bank, dry cleaning slip – the list goes on. You just
need a wooden clothes peg and some double-sided
adhesive tape. If you want, you can paint or decorate
the peg. Cut out a piece of fabric, patterned paper or
wallpaper and fix to the front of the peg using double-
sided tape – or just leave it plain. Fix to the door, or
a convenient spot you can't miss on your way out.
So simple but life changing!

A few simple ways to never lose your keys

How many times have you been ready to leave the house when you suddenly realise you have no idea where your keys are? A total nightmare. The school run's the worst. You finally get out of the house and then realise that while you've been focusing on piling the kids into the car you've absent-mindedly put your keys somewhere. A pocket? In your jacket? Trousers? The bottom of your bag? Cue frantic patting of every pocket and highly undignified tipping out of jumbled contents of bag in the street. I'm kind of hoping you recognise this and that it's not just me. Well anyway, having endured this too many times, I finally hit upon some ultra-simple solutions.

Keep them round your neck

Attach a long loop of fabric or ribbon to your keys, so that you can wear them like a necklace. Not all the time, obviously, just when you're going in and out of the house or to and from the car. The simplest way to do this is to cut a strip of fabric measuring 90 x 3cm, or a length of ribbon. Thread it through your keys and knot the ends together tightly. If you have an especially cavernous handbag, you can loop it onto the bag handle before putting your keys inside. Now you can easily fish them back out of the murky depths. Joyous.

Always keep them in one place at home

The best way to keep track of your keys in the house is to put a little hook on the inside of a cupboard fairly near the front door. For security reasons you don't want it to be obvious or in view. I wouldn't hang a key box close to the front door, for instance – stylish as it might look. You want the keys hidden away but handy. Now get in the habit of always putting them on the hook the moment you come through the door, and you'll never lose them again.

Label all the house keys

Numerous house keys, bike keys and various spares tend to accumulate and get stashed together in a forgotten jumble. A little time spent labelling them up will pay back over and again in saved time and stress if you ever lose a key. I was moved to label all our household keys when we lost a vital door key and I spent hours stressed out looking everywhere for it – trying to get inside the head of a two-year-old (the likely culprit) to think where she might have put it – inside every drawer, every shoe, every toy box, the bin – all her usual favourite hiding places. After a lot of wasted time searching I suddenly remembered there might be a spare lurking in our hellish box of jumbled keys. After working my way through several, finally – eureka! So, to prevent the same thing happening again, I made up large laminated labels for all our keys.

Here's how to do it. You need paper – any colour you like – a stamper set (or a nice chunky felt-tip) and some credit card-sized self-laminating pouches. Stamp or write your word on the card, and cut out around it. Hold the card against the laminating pouch to check it will fit in – you should actually be able to fit two labels into each one. Stick one or two into the self-laminating pouch and then cut around. Punch a hole, thread string or ribbon through, attach your keys, and voilà – they look funky too! Aah, don't you just love those jobs that, once done, don't need to be done again and again, unlike the cooking, the washing, the cleaning....

PAINT A CHALKBOARD

A blackboard diary is a very simple way of keeping track of what's going on in a busy household over the week – everyone can note down what they're up to, or what needs to be bought if it's running out. Buy some blackboard paint from any hardware or DIY store, block out your space on the wall using masking tape, and paint. You'll need two or three coats to get a really good covering. Be careful when you peel off the masking tape because the paint is very thick, so the tape might lift off little bits of paint around the edges. If that happens, just re-mask and touch up where necessary. Anywhere in or near the kitchen is good. If there's no obvious spot, and you don't want it to be a feature of the room, you could even paint it on the back of the kitchen door, which a friend of mine has done and it works brilliantly. My chalkboard is 76 x 60cm, which is a good practical size for this, but just work with the space you've got.

DO THINGS STRAIGHT AWAY

If you need to make a call, send a letter or email, or arrange something, try do it at once – unless there is a really good reason not to. Then you can forget about it and it takes the least amount of time and headspace. When you know you've got to do something but never quite get round to it, it becomes a hassle. When I was about nine I had a teacher who was practically Edwardian and used to bellow at us: 'Procrastination is a waste of time!'. I had absolutely no idea what he meant then. It took me many years and lots of wasted time to finally get what he meant. And it is completely true. Next time an email or text or anything else requiring your attention comes in, deal with it immediately. Job done.

CUT OUT THE JUNK

Junk mail can overwhelm your mailbox, so you lose sight of emails that are actually important and need to be dealt with. Getting rid of the junk mail allows you to focus. Luckily it's incredibly easy to sort. Just open up the email and scroll to the bottom where you will find a section that says 'unsubscribe' in tiny print and 'click here'. It will redirect you to a page that automatically takes you off the mailing list. Get in the habit of doing this every time something you don't want comes through. It's so much more satisfying to open your mail box and not have to wade through all the junk to see if there's something you actually want in there. To keep track of emails, delete anything you don't need as soon as you've read it. If there's important information in an email that you need to keep for reference – like a holiday booking – print and file it.

WHEN YOU MAKE AN APPOINTMENT, BOOK AROUND IT

If, for example, the appointment means that you need a babysitter, book one there and then. If it's too far ahead for the babysitter to commit, stick a reminder note in your diary several weeks before the date so you don't forget to ask again and risk having to scramble at the last minute desperately trying to find someone – anyone. If the diary date is a big event and you think you'll want a blow-dry or haircut on the day, book it straight away. If it's a wedding invitation, or similar, and means an overnight stay, book the accommodation immediately. If you've a pet that needs to be checked in for an overnight stay somewhere, again do it right away. None of this is extra effort; it's less effort and stress in the long run.

Start the day with a clear head
by getting up before everyone else.

BUY AN EXTRA HOUR IN THE DAY

I suggest this because it's a trick I picked up from some of the most successful people I know, but I'm afraid you might not like it. Basically you have to get up an hour before anyone else. I know you probably already feel like you don't get enough sleep, but let me explain why this really is worth doing. When you get up at the same time as everyone else, your day starts with the juggling act of getting everyone ready for the school run and you begin feeling like things are running beyond your control. By getting up before the chaos begins, you avert that by buying yourself breathing space. If you're trying to do a project that you never seem to find the time for – like writing a book, or sorting out photographs – this is the perfect time to do it. Or you could do some exercise – even go out for a run – no worries about childcare while kids and partner are asleep! When the alarm goes off and you don't actually have to get up, the temptation just to roll over and go back to sleep is immense, but I promise you, when you've done it once you'll want to do it again. Even if you just get up half an hour or twenty minutes before everyone else, it makes a difference. You don't need to do it every day (and almost certainly not at weekends), but it is a counter-intuitive way of helping to restore your equilibrium.

LIGHTEN THE LOAD OF CHILDCARE BY SETTING UP A TRADING SYSTEM WITH FRIENDS

The cost of childcare can be horribly expensive, so the upshot can be that nights out alone for you and your partner just don't happen anymore. Spending time together when you can actually chat, rather than hunker down on the sofa watching TV, is really important, so don't let the expense of a sitter stop you doing it. Why not get together with a group of friends and set up a system where you trade your time? Do it on an hourly basis, so that it is completely fair and everyone gets back the hours they give. You could expand this and agree childcare swaps, where you have someone else's children for a few hours, a day or even overnight, and they have yours in return for the same period of time. The prospect of doubling the number of kids to look after might put you off, but actually it can be easier to look after your own kids when others are around because they don't keep asking to be entertained – they seem to get together and play much better. The upside is a clear period for you without children to do whatever you want. Lush.

KEEP A BOOK FOR GREAT CHILDCARE COMMUNICATIONS

If you have a nanny or anyone else looking after your children while you work, it's often a case of passing ships – she steams in as you steam out, and there's little time for communication. To make your life easier, get a book so that anything that should be passed on can be written down, and not forgotten about. Make notes in 'The Book' of anything you should know about, anything you need to buy, anything bothering the nanny or the children, anything great or funny – anything! Likewise, if you need to tell the carer about a holiday date, or other arrangement, make a note as soon as you think of it. That way she can see it if you forget to tell her, which (if you're like me) no doubt you will. Note down all contact numbers in the book too. If your carer doesn't drive, include the contact number for a taxi company which you know and trust, which has child car seats and will allow you to pay over the phone, so in the event of an emergency you know she and the kids can safely get somewhere.

KEEP TRACK OF PAPERWORK

As someone who goes in fits and bursts of being on top of paperwork, this is the best system I've found for at least having it in an organised state for when I do find the time to sit down and sort it. You need three box files: one for receipts; one for stuff that needs to be filed; and one for stuff that needs to be dealt with. When letters come in, just stick them in the correct boxes. Try to set aside twenty minutes one morning a week to go through the boxes and deal with it all. Provided you do a little and often, it won't pile up and overwhelm you. Buy the cheapest plain box files you can (see page 129 for how to customise them very easily). You could, of course, leave them plain, but I do think it's more appealing to do a tedious job when you've got something pretty to admire at the same time.

ORGANISE INSTRUCTION MANUALS
AND RELATED PARAPHERNALIA

When you buy a new piece of kit – a camera, a printer, or anything else – it always comes with a whole stack of paperwork and little accoutrements. You know you should keep them, but invariably they end up getting tucked away somewhere that you instantly forget about. If you do ever actually need to retrieve the relevant documents, then hunting them down takes ages. Next time you buy something new, put anything you need to keep in a resealable plastic bag and write on the front what it's for. Then keep it in a big envelope, in a drawer, box or cupboard, specifically designated for instruction manuals. When you replace something, don't forget to remove defunct paperwork, to stay on top of clutter. Super satisfying.

TROUBLESHOOT YOUR PROBLEMS:
REMEMBER, SOMETIMES THE SIMPLEST THING
CAN MAKE THE BIGGEST DIFFERENCE

We all live with things that really annoy us – and I'm not talking other people here – I mean the constantly dripping tap, the fact that there's never any bread when you want it, etc, etc. Actually, we could easily resolve most of these annoyances in minutes if we just stopped for a moment to focus. One of my little bugbears was a permanent gap between the bedroom curtains when they were closed at night, which meant a streetlight was shining right in my eyes. After living with it for months I suddenly realised one morning I could just hold it shut with a safety pin. Why did that take so long? So next time something bothers you, write it down – keep a page in a notebook for the annoyances. Once you've written it down, it helps you to think about a strategy to deal with it. The bread problem, for instance. Once I focused on it I realised there was a blindingly simple solution – keep bread in the freezer. With the dripping tap, you could read up about how to change a washer yourself, or just keep a running list of little jobs around the house that you can't do, and get a handyman in for a day to crack through them.

SCHEDULE TIME IN THE DIARY FOR JOBS

When you know you've got a really boring chore to do – like sorting out car insurance – why not book a slot in the diary to get it done – just like you're running a business. It means it's not hanging over you like a ghoul every day, making you feel guilty because you know you should sort it, but never quite seem to get around to it. Forget all about it until the allotted time comes, then crack through it in the scheduled hour. Now put your feet up, satisfied, job done.

GET THE DREADED ALL-DAY CALL-OUT TO WORK AROUND YOU

I guess companies still do this, just because they can. Presumably they wouldn't if the person at the top had ever experienced the frustration of a wasted day spent killing time at home, racing in and out for the school run as quickly as possible, watching the clock, waiting, only for the engineer to arrive a minute before the end of the allotted time frame. Grrrrrr. There are two ways to manage this. First, if you can, book a scheduled appointment – like a boiler service – for the school holidays. That way you don't have to panic about the engineer arriving just as you've left the house for the school run. Instead you (or whoever's looking after the kids) can relax into a lazy and luxurious pyjama day doing puzzles, watching a movie and baking cookies. Alternatively, always ask for the engineer to call when they're half an hour away – invariably they won't offer to do it, but most companies will if you ask nicely.

Never again have to hang around, wasting precious time, waiting in for a call-out or delivery.

★ **Wonder Tip** ★

Shopping online is brilliant for sooooooo many reasons – the downside is having to wait in for a parcel. Obviously you can have an arrangement with neighbours to take in each other's deliveries, but it's not always convenient. The life changer for me was getting an outdoor parcel box that takes really big packages and can be locked securely by the postman with no need for a key. Just stick a little note by the doorbell and show anyone who makes regular deliveries to your home how it works. No more time wasted waiting in for a delivery that you can guarantee will come the moment you step out of the house. Liberating!

Getting Organized
FOR BIG EVENTS

Planning is vital when it comes to high days and holidays. Whether you want to book a trip, a restaurant, tickets, a venue, an entertainer or anything else, just do it early. The beauty of things like birthdays, anniversaries and Christmas is that the dates don't ever change. It's not like they suddenly spring up and surprise you. (Well, unless you've forgotten, of course, but hopefully with a little organisation, you won't forget important dates again!) If you have a great idea for a special occasion, book it as early as you can. That way you will have the best tickets, the restaurant table you want, the party when and where you want it, etc. A great way of making sure you get tickets to shows, concerts and events, without having to pay way over face value for resale tickets, is to sign up for listing alerts, so you're one of the first to know when tickets go on sale.

HOW NOT TO FORGET A BIRTHDAY AGAIN
The strategy here goes back to the most basic one – write everything down. When you get your new diary go through the old one and copy over any important dates – birthdays, anniversaries, etc. Having been far too bad for far too long at remembering birthdays, I've now got a belt and braces policy. On top of the diary reminders I have a brilliant phone app where I list all birthdays and it works as a countdown, telling me whose birthday is coming up next, how many days away it is, and how old the person is going to be. The age thing is especially useful because I find it almost impossible to remember how old everyone is, which can be particularly problematic when you're trying to work out whether a present is age appropriate for a child.

PRESENT PLANNER
It's a great idea to stock up on presents when you see them – especially if it's at sale time when you can get a much bigger bang for your buck. That said, beware of buying stuff without thinking specifically who you will give it to. It's a false economy and those things can end up lurking in a cupboard. Keep a book where you write down presents as you buy them, as well as gift ideas as you think of them. It's really annoying when inspiration strikes months before someone's birthday – you're sure you won't forget, but of course, once the birthday finally comes around, you can guarantee that the thought has simply evaporated without trace.

KEEP A PRESENT BOX OR DRAWER...
...or cupboard – just somewhere to put any gifts when you buy them, so that you can easily find them again.

See pages 184–187 for a countdown to Christmas and gear up for the big day in small, simple, stress-free steps.

Keeping
HOUSE

BEFORE WE GO ON, I should say that I have not deliberately sought out eco-friendly cleaning methods. For a long time I actually shied away from home-made cleaning products, thinking the effort of sourcing the items required and the faff of mixing them up would be more hassle than it was worth. I ABSOLUTELY promise you that is not the case. For a start, all of the items can be bought very easily in a supermarket, hardware store, or (invariably most cheaply and in bulk) online. They are much, much cheaper than the products that line supermarket shelves, making you believe you need to fill your own cupboards with task-specific expensive products. And they genuinely work just as well, or – more often than not – better, than chemical products. Armed with empty bottles, spray bottles and jars, you can label up your home-made products so that they look stylishly utilitarian into the bargain.

Keeping House

WITH MINIMUM EFFORT
AND MAXIMUM RETURN

THIS IS MY LIST OF
INDISPENSABLE HOUSEHOLD ITEMS:

- **Bicarbonate of soda** My number one hero product. Buy in bulk online.
- **Soda crystals** You'll find them hidden away on the bottom shelf in the laundry section of the supermarket – or buy online.
- **Bleach**
- **Scouring cream**
- **White vinegar** (otherwise known as distilled malt vinegar)
- **A big bowl of lemons**
- **A roll of multi-purpose cloths** Cheap and disposable, so no more wasting time trying to clean a filthy or bacteria-ridden cloth. One will last for days of simple wipe-downs, but if you're doing a job like cleaning the oven, it's a guilt-free one-hit wonder.
- **Microfibre cloths** LOVE, LOVE, LOVE them!
- **Bag clips** Use to reseal all packaging to prevent spillages, and also to keep things fresh.
- **Metal scourer** Those ones that look like rolled up metal springs; not the ones like wire wool, which are horrid to use.

- **A great vacuum cleaner** By which I mean a powerful 2000-watt compact cleaner; not an upright, which is a nightmare to haul up and down stairs.
- **A stack of plastic trugs** A lifesaver when it comes to lugging piles of laundry or anything else around the house.
- **Empty spray bottles** Keep and reuse all old spray bottles.
- **Wood and natural bristle washing-up brushes** Good brushes are worth investing in because they last forever, and so work out much cheaper than plastic ones in the long run. They also somehow make doing the washing-up more pleasurable just because they look so lovely. Keep them in a pretty jug by the sink so they are always to hand and look stylish to boot. A glass brush (which is like a ball of soft bristles) is especially excellent when it comes to washing glasses (duh!), bottles and jars.
- **Always keep old toothbrushes for cleaning** Brilliant for getting into tight spots and for cleaning jewellery.

Why spend more money than you have to on the boring stuff? Using these simple basics will save you a small fortune on expensive products.

The
BATHROOM

KEEP YOUR SHOWER DOOR SPARKLING WITHOUT EVER HAVING TO CLEAN IT

Here is a really neat trick to keep your shower door and walls clean and sparkling with practically zero effort. You just need a window cleaner's scraper. Use it to wipe down the walls after each shower. I used to spend a fortune on shower sprays until I discovered this. It is a total bargain and the most efficient way to stop water runs leaving limescale marks all over the walls and glass, which look hideous and are a total chore to get rid of. You can buy a scraper anywhere – most supermarkets sell them. Just get in the habit of running it over the glass and walls before you get out of the shower. Make sure anyone else who takes a shower does it too. One arduous job totally eliminated. Fabulous!

SAVE YOURSELF FROM EVER SPENDING TIME CLEANING MOULD AND MILDEW

The combination of warmth and water in a bathroom makes it a perfect breeding ground for mould, so make sure water isn't pooling behind bottles of shampoo and shower gel. When you go over the glass and walls with the shower scraper, make sure you swipe all the water off the ledges of the bath or tiles. Doing this (which takes seconds) should save you ever having to deal with those little spots of black mildew or strange orangey mould that develops in bathrooms. Another job avoided. Yay!

IF YOU'VE GOT MILDEW, GET RID OF IT WITH MINIMUM EFFORT

If you already have mildew or mould – don't worry; it's really common and luckily it's not difficult to get rid of it. It takes a while because you have to leave bleach to work on it for several hours, but it's not arduous. Just paint bleach onto any mildewed areas using an old toothbrush. Leave for around three hours while the bleach kills the mildew off. Before rinsing the bleach away, scrub at a bit of the mildew with the toothbrush to check it will come away easily. If not, leave for a bit longer, otherwise wipe away the bleach with a disposable cloth and then clean well with plenty of water. Dry thoroughly.

NEVER CLEAN THE BATHROOM MIRROR AGAIN

If you spatter anything on the mirror, always wipe it away instantly. It's so much quicker and easier to clean anything before it's dried and set. Either use a towel, or keep a microfibre cloth in the bathroom.

AVOID THE FULL BATHROOM CLEAN, WITH A QUICK WIPE DOWN, LITTLE AND OFTEN

When a towel's ready for the wash, use it to give everything a quick wipe-down before you put it in the washing box. Run the towel around the bath and sink and give the taps a quick buff. It takes seconds, but keeps the bathroom looking clean and fresh all the time – and saves you ever having to clean a *really* dirty bathroom.

CLEAN THE BATH AND SINK IN SECONDS

If you're in the habit of giving the bath and sink a quick daily wipe, you shouldn't ever get to the stage of having to clean away full-scale scum – euuww. Just use a little scouring cream on a damp cloth and wipe over all the surfaces, then rinse away and dry. Easy.

STOP PIPES GETTING BLOCKED WITH HAIR

A blocked sink or bath is a total hassle, and fairly gruesome to deal with. The doubly annoying thing is, you've probably unwittingly caused it to happen in the first place. The main reason for the pipes blocking is hair accumulating under the plughole and getting gummed up with soap and shampoo. Yuk. Luckily, it's easy to avoid. Get a special little sieve that lies over the plughole to stop hair going down it. Buy in any hardware store or online. Job averted, and loads of money saved on heavy-duty chemicals.

MAXIMISE THE POWER OF YOUR SHOWER

Limescale builds up in shower heads, especially if you live in a hard-water area, and the blockages stop the water flowing fully. So whenever you see limescale crusting on the holes of the shower head, it's worth descaling it. If it will unscrew, remove the shower head. This makes the job super easy. Just put it in a bowl of white vinegar and leave for a couple of hours. If the shower head doesn't unscrew, use the same bag trick as with taps (see below).

GET RID OF LIMESCALE ON TAPS

Limescale can build up around the opening of taps. It doesn't do any harm; it just doesn't look fab. Let's face it though, as it's not an urgent task and doesn't affect the performance of the taps, it never quite makes it to the top of the chores list. However, getting rid of it is so easy, the job practically does itself. Put about a tablespoon's worth of vinegar in a non-leaky plastic bag and strap it over the spout, securing it to the tap with an elastic band. Do this when you are not going to need the tap for a while, as it takes a couple of hours for the vinegar to completely dissolve the limescale. No scrubbing for you.

GET SUPER-SHINY TAPS

Mix up the juice of half a lemon with a teaspoon of bicarb. Apply with a toothbrush to get in all the nooks and crannies. Rinse off with plenty of water. Buff dry with a microfibre cloth, and the taps will be shinier than you have ever seen them.

SAVE A FORTUNE ON SHAMPOO BY INVESTING IN A FOAMING PUMP DISPENSER

Buy a pump dispenser, which magically converts liquid to foam. You put a little shampoo in the bottle, top up with water, and when you press on the pump it dispenses foam. This is great for two reasons. It will save you loads of money spent on shampoo, because it prolongs the life of one bottle many times over. And it means you don't use too much shampoo when washing your hair (see page 92).

ZERO-EFFORT LOO CLEANING

First of all, you need a good brush, for arms-length cleaning. The quickest and easiest way to keep a loo sparkling and germ free is to squirt bleach down it and under the rim twice a week. If you don't want to use bleach, or can't because of a septic tank, trusty old bicarb and vinegar are a good alternative. Just sprinkle bicarb into the water and around the bowl and spray over white vinegar and lemon juice so that it fizzes. (Keep a spray of 250ml vinegar plus the juice of a lemon – sieved to get rid of pith – for general cleaning.) Use the loo brush to scrub some up under the brim and then leave for as long as you can. When you flush, the loo will be spangly. Use a disposable cloth and the vinegar/lemon spray to wipe under the seat and behind the lid.

GET A BRAND SPANGLY NEW-LOOKING TOILET BY CLEANING AWAY A BUILD-UP OF LIMESCALE

A build-up of limescale in the loo looks gruesome, but getting rid of it is actually very easy because it's another classic case of leaving the job to do itself. It requires a little effort on your part first of all, because you need to suction out as much water as possible from the toilet bowl. Use a plunger and pump it up and down over the water until most of it has been forced out. Apply a limescale remover directly onto the surfaces of the bowl where limescale has built up. Squirt a generous amount into the water to work on anywhere that is still submerged. Leave it for as long as you can. Overnight is great. Before flushing, give the surfaces a good scrub with a loo brush. It is possible to restore even the most irredeemable-looking loo to pristine condition this way. If you can't use chemical products or bleach because of a septic tank,

suction out the water, sprinkle bicarb liberally over the limescale, spritz with vinegar, and leave overnight as before. It might not take it all off in one go, so you might need to repeat this. We had one loo that was so gross I thought it wasn't worth trying to tackle, and figured we'd have to replace it some time. Eventually I got round to sorting it out, and it now looks like new. A fortune saved in not having to spend money on something as ultimately boring as a new loo. Hoorah!

HOW TO UNBLOCK THE LOO

All you need is a plunger. Put it on your shopping list if you haven't got one already – they're cheap and you never know when you might need it! Place it directly over the opening where everything's flushed away, press down firmly and pull away sharply. Do this as many times as you need for the blockage to be dislodged and normality restored. Phew.

CLEAN FLOOR TILES AND DIRTY GROUTING

The quickest and easiest way to do this is with a scouring cream on a damp cloth plus a little bit of elbow grease.

CLEAN THE PULL CORD IN THREE SECONDS FLAT

The pull cord on bathroom lights looks pretty grim when it gets grubby at the bottom where you pull on it. Don't cut it ever shorter, until you have to replace it. Just get a little bleach on a damp cloth, hold it round the cord and rub the cloth up and down a few times. In just seconds, the cord will be miraculously restored to dazzling whiteness. A small thing, but it does make a difference.

The
KITCHEN

CLEAN GLASS, MIRRORS, WINDOWS AND STAINLESS STEEL IN SECONDS

Microfibre cloths are the way to go! They are genius. They get rid of the need to use any chemical sprays – good for the environment, yes, tick, but selfishly I'm more interested in what they mean in terms of saving time and money. You can clean mirrors, glass and stainless steel in seconds with one of these.

If you just need to remove smears, a brisk rub with the cloth should be enough. If the marks are sticky then go over first with a damp cloth and then buff up. The cloths aren't always cheap (buy online or in a supermarket – any brand will do), but after the initial outlay that's it. You don't need to buy other cleaning products for any of these jobs –

and the cloths last forever. There are several different types of microfibre cloth – go for the soft, fluffy ones, which work brilliantly on all surfaces more effectively than the smooth woven cloths. A truly life-changing discovery. No more heart-sinking moments when you see sticky fingerprints all over the fridge or a mirror – you'll have them cleaned off in seconds!

CLEAN THE INSIDE OF THE FRIDGE WITH A QUICK SPRITZ OF VINEGAR AND ZERO EFFORT

It's good to get in the habit of keeping the fridge clean and well ordered because then you don't overload it with stuff that gets forgotten until you smell the whiff after it's gone off. A small amount of effort on this front will save lots of money, as you won't be throwing out food you've bought but forgotten to eat. You may just as well have put that cash straight in the bin. So before you go to the supermarket, rifle through the shelves to see what you've got. While you're at it, give each shelf a quick spritz with a vinegar spray. Wipe down with a tea towel and suddenly everything looks so much brighter and more appealing.

DEODORISE THE FRIDGE WITH A LEMON

Half a lemon in the fridge is an amazing thing! It will completely get rid of all bad smells, even from the stinkiest of cheeses. I don't know how it works, but it really does. Change the lemon every couple of months and you don't ever need to worry about fridge pongs again!

CLEANING THE KITCHEN FLOOR

I have struggled with working out a corner-cutting method for cleaning the floor. The problem is, mops save your back, but I've never found one that actually gets the floor as clean as doing the job on your hands and knees. Why does it matter? Well, the problem with floors is that if they're not properly clean, the dirt gets ingrained when people walk over them, and then they look shabby and are really hard to get clean. So...

...**once a fortnight** get down on your hands and knees to give the floor a really good clean. Put a couple of tea towels under your knees to protect your clothes (or skin, if you're doing this in hot weather!) Always give the floor a good sweep first. In a bowl mix up a solution of the juice of half a lemon, 1 cup of white vinegar and 1 cup of warm water. Get another bowl of warm water and a couple of cloths. Alternate the cleaning cloths (when one is dirty, put it in the bowl of water and let it soak clean while you use the other, and so on). Wring the cloth out well, so it is just slightly damp, then put it in the lemon and vinegar solution, squeeze out the excess and get scrubbing. This method works brilliantly on most surfaces. If you have a wooden floor, add two teaspoons of olive oil to the mix.

...**once a week** go over the floor with a mop. Again, always sweep or vacuum first. Make the cleaning solution more dilute, so mix the juice of 1 lemon, 2 cups of vinegar and 4 cups of water in a bucket. Don't forget the oil for wooden floors.

GET AN EVERLASTING BOTTLE OF WASHING-UP LIQUID

Well, that's a slight exaggeration, it might not last you forever, but here is a brilliant way of making your washing-up liquid last probably around a hundred (er, that's a guess, not a scientifically proven statistic) times longer than normal. Anyway, buy a foaming soap dispenser. These things are genius! Basically you put a small amount of liquid soap in the container, then fill it up with water. The pump magically transforms the liquid into foam as it is dispensed, so you use a lot less of it than when you liberally splash it out of the bottle. Also, it looks much nicer than a horrible old bottle of washing-up liquid sitting on the side.

STOCK UP ON TEA TOWELS

An enormous pile of tea towels is vital in the kitchen, so that you always have fresh dry ones to hand. Curiously, it's a basic that feels like a luxury. I don't know why, but there seems to be a universal sense that three will suffice. For years I had three and too often found myself desperately trying to dry up with a useless soggy rag. Then I went through a phase of spending a small fortune on kitchen roll, which I'd lavish on the drying up. Until I suddenly thought, 'Why three? Why not ten?' A pile of tea towels is one of those small but life-changing things.

And tea towels are great for covering food to keep it warm, because they keep heat in while absorbing steam, so that the food doesn't go soggy.

When you've washed tea towels, stretch them out and dry naturally. They will dry stiff, which makes them more absorbent.

EASY-PEASY LEMON SQUEEZY OVEN CLEANING

Forget any of the specialist products that line supermarket shelves, dazzling you into thinking you need to spend a small fortune on something so boring. Hmmm, a fiver on oven cleaner or a new lipstick. What do you think? All you need is some steam, some lemon juice, and possibly a little brilliant, and brilliantly cheap, bicarbonate of soda. Turn on the oven for twenty minutes to get it to top temperature. Get an ovenproof bowl, squeeze in the juice of half a lemon and boil the kettle. When the oven's hot, turn it off. Pour the boiling water in with the lemon juice, put it in the oven and leave it to steam for half an hour.

Use a damp cloth to wipe the oven as clean as you can. Use a metal scourer on areas that need extra muscle. This should be enough to get the oven spangly. If it's really encrusted and you do need something more to cut through the grime, mix up two teaspoons of bicarbonate and the juice from the other half of the lemon, apply, leave for a few minutes, then scrub. Make sure you remove all the bicarb residue with a damp cloth or it will leave white streaks. Buff up with a cloth and your oven will sparkle like new! I once paid someone to come and clean my oven professionally. I don't think he was very good, but anyway, he didn't do it as well as this! By the way, lest you think I am a total clean freak, there is a very practical reason for keeping your oven clean – it avoids the clouds of acrid smoke that billow out of a dirty oven every time you turn it on.

LET THE KETTLE CLEAN ITSELF

If you have a metal kettle, the easiest and quickest way to get it looking as shiny as new is to give it a quick buff with a tea towel when it's just boiled.

How to clean the hob

First, remove anything that will go into the dishwasher and put on a hot wash. Now make up a strong solution using ½ cupful of bicarb to ½ cupful of hot water. Put the paste over all areas where grease and food residue are encrusted. Leave for thirty minutes. The bicarb totally cuts through any grease and should remove all but the dirt that has been spot welded on, thanks to recurrent high heat. Use a disposable cloth to wipe clean. To get rid of anything left behind, sprinkle bicarb directly onto the area and spritz vinegar or lemon juice over, so that it fizzes up. Leave for twenty minutes or so. Then use a damp cloth to scrub away. If it's still not shifting as well as you'd like, unleash the metal scourer. The combination should remove even the most ancient layers of burnt on residue with little effort.

Don't forget the extractor hood

This is where all the steam and smoke from cooking goes, so it's not surprising that it gets pretty disgusting. Because it's out of sight it's easy to forget the sticky grime building up just above your head. I don't want to make extra work out of something that could easily go unnoticed, but it is important to give it a good clean at least once a year, because if the filters are blocked, they won't do the job properly. Anyway, it's not arduous to do. The metal grease filters should pop out very easily. Put them in the dishwasher to get them as clean as new. If you don't have a dishwasher, leave them to soak for at least half an hour in hot, soapy water, with a cupful of bicarbonate of soda, before scrubbing clean with a stiff brush. If you have an extractor that re-circulates the air, rather than venting it to the outside, you should replace the carbon filters too.

Prevent blocked pipes

Prevention is always so much better than cure. To save yourself the hassle of blocked drains, keep the plughole in the kitchen sink covered with a special strainer to stop anything that might block the pipes. Buy in any hardware store.

Avoid a drain disaster

If you ever accidentally pour fat down the kitchen sink you can avoid a blocked U-bend by instantly swishing half a pack of soda crystals after it, followed by boiling water. That should be enough to degrease the pipes. If not…

…here's how to unblock a U-bend

It's not a pleasant job, but it is easy to do. First, remove as much water from the blocked sink as you can. Then put an empty bucket below the U-bend and unscrew the two plastic collars that attach it to the straight pipes. Drop the U-bend into the bucket and let any excess water flow in with it. If the blockage is between the plughole and the U-bend, use something like the handle of a wooden spoon to force it clear. If the blockage is in the U-bend, clean it thoroughly in soda crystals and hot water to degrease and unblock. Once it's completely clear, screw it back in place and make yourself a nice cup of tea. Builder's of course. Jubbly.

Use an upright dustpan and brush

Keeping the kitchen floor and under the table clear of crumbs and any other dropped food is pretty basic if you don't want mice, ants or other pests. To make the job as quick and easy as possible, and save your back, get a long-handled dustpan and brush.

How to descale the kettle

Pour 200ml of white vinegar, plus the juice of half a lemon, into the kettle. Boil it, then leave for as long as you can. The majority of the limescale will be removed within five to ten minutes, but if the limescale is bad, leave it for at least half an hour, or even overnight. Rinse out well before using. The beauty of using lemon and vinegar is you don't need to worry about horrible chemicals in your kettle.

How to de-ice a freezer

First, turn off the freezer. Transfer the contents to freezer bags, if you have some. If not, use regular bags and pack everything together. Sprinkle salt over the ice – it makes it melt quickly. Put a towel on the floor to protect it from any water that might leak out – and to save you having to mop it up. After about five minutes the ice should have be thawing enough for you to start chipping away. Don't be brutal though – you don't want to damage any vital components under the ice. Use something blunt like an old credit card as a scraper. Scrape the ice onto a tray – much easier than using a bowl or bucket because it lies flat. Make sure the inside of the freezer is completely dry before you turn it back on and restock.

Have a good clear-out

Don't you find it extraordinary how quickly stuff accumulates in cupboards? Before you know it, you have no idea what's actually lurking inside. A jam-packed kitchen cupboard should mean it's stashed full of food that you can actually eat. Instead, what it invariably means is that it's full of stuff you've forgotten you have. So don't forget to have a good clear-out of the cupboards every six months or so.

That way you know what you've got and actually use it. And it's so much nicer for your soul when you open a door onto a well-organised space, rather than a cluttered hellhole. Same with the fridge and freezer – make sure they don't become graveyards for food that you buy with the best intentions but then promptly forget all about.

Simplify and streamline
with a bit of labelling

When you've emptied out all the rubbish from a cupboard, to try to avoid clutter quickly accumulating again, decant packets into glass jars and label them up, so that you can quickly and easily see what you've got and what you're running out of. That way you won't keep buying stuff you've already got.

Opening jars without having a hernia

Don't huff and puff and go red in the face while you battle with a hermetically sealed lid. Just bang firmly all around the edge of it with a blunt knife. It should break the seal so that the lid screws off easily. If it won't come off because the contents have spilt over the lip of the jar, effectively gluing the lid on, run it under the hot tap for twenty seconds or so, and you should then be able to twist off the lid with no sweat.

★ *Wonder Tip* ★

Incidentally, if you have a hard lemon (either unripe, or old and dehydrated), cut it in half and microwave it for twenty seconds. Now you'll be able to juice it easily!

Food

THE GADGETS

It's difficult to know which kitchen gadgets are worth investing in and which will just languish in a drawer unused – an annoying reminder for evermore of money wasted. But when you do happen upon something that really does do what it says on the tin it can be life changing. So here's my very quick guide to things I think really are worth the investment:

- **A fine grater** A wonder tool for preparing garlic and ginger. It is so much easier and quicker than a garlic press, which is unwieldy and flattens and wastes a large portion of the clove. This grates the garlic into a paste that will disperse and absorb perfectly into whatever you're cooking. It also makes using ginger a revelation. I used to hate having to put ginger in a recipe because I could never chop it finely enough, but with the grater it's transformed into a perfect paste with no effort at all. A slight warning: the reason it works so well is that the grating side is very sharp, so you do have to be a bit careful using it. And do store it in the casing it came in.

- **A great lemon squeezer** Having tried practically every lemon squeezer on the market, the design I really recommend is a hand-held contraption that you slot half a lemon into face down. Press until every last drop of juice is squeezed out through small holes, without pips. Use it for limes too. Easy to clean and super quick and easy to use.
- **Silicone oven mitts** They will completely protect your hand and arms, won't get singed and ruined in the oven, and you can just stick them in the dishwasher when they're dirty. An all-round hero design.
- **A pizza wheel** Because kids love pizza, and cutting it up into slices without one is a faff – this does the job in two seconds flat.
- **Good tongs** Invaluable for serving anything and everything.

Wonder Tip

Put your old garlic presser to use as a hair maker for children's playdough instead; they'll love it!

Build up a good set of knives: a chef's knife, a bread knife, a paring knife and a carving knife... and keep them sharp (see page 47 for tips)

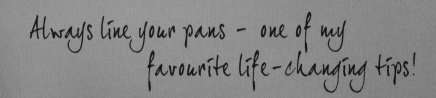

Always line your pans — one of my
favourite life-changing tips!

NEVER SCRUB A PAN AGAIN

This is one of those 'why didn't I think of that before?' tips, which you will be grateful for every time you cook and don't have to scrub the pan afterwards! Just line the cooking tin with non-stick baking paper before using it. Get in the habit of doing it every time, whatever you're cooking. Roast potatoes, fish fingers, roast meat, cookies – anything and everything. It doesn't affect the cooking but will save hours of scrubbing.

SAVE YOURSELF A WHOLE LOAD OF WASHING-UP WHEN YOU'RE COOKING

Invest in a set of electronic scales that measure liquids and solids. Just put your mixing bowl on top and zero and change the setting each time you add something, depending on whether you need to measure out liquid or solid. No need to get loads of measuring jugs or bowls dirty. Utter genius.

LET THE MICROWAVE CLEAN ITSELF

Squeeze the juice of a lemon into a bowl and add an equal quantity of water. Microwave on full power for five minutes. The lemony steam will rehydrate any hardened food splashes or deposits, so a quick wipe with a damp cloth is all that is needed to get it back to mint condition. If the dirt doesn't wipe away easily, zap for another five minutes.

DEODORISE A STINKY MICROWAVE

If you've microwaved something stinky, just chuck in half a lemon when the food's done and microwave for a minute. It will absorb the smell, and leave it lemon fresh. Phew.

USE LEMON JUICE AS A NATURAL PRESERVATIVE FOR CUT FRUIT TO STOP IT GOING BROWN OR DEHYDRATING.

It works especially brilliantly on apples, cucumber, strawberries and avocadoes. Just squeeze over liberally as soon as you have chopped the fruit. It means you can prepare in advance and leftovers will keep in the fridge – hooray!

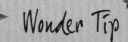

Wonder Tip

When you've been chopping garlic, onions, chillies, or anything else stinky, get rid of the smell by squishing your fingers into the flesh of a cut lemon. Get the juice all over your fingers and rub them together before rinsing away with cold water. Fragrance restored.

FREEZE SLICED BREAD

This is literally the best thing since sliced bread –
especially if you have to make packed lunches every
morning. In the freezer, a loaf of bread will last as
long as you want it to, so you don't get to that stage
where you're trying to scrape off little green bits,
hoping it won't matter, or making sandwiches from
hard, stale bread. You can stock up with several
loaves at a time, so you're not always having to
remember to buy it. And, maybe best of all, spreading
anything on frozen slices is a cinch – even butter
straight out of the fridge, or marmite, won't tear it.
Don't worry – it defrosts back to its natural fresh
state in about ten minutes. Freezing is also brilliant
for delicious freshly baked loaves, which only ever
last a day before going rock hard. Slice as soon as
you get home and freeze in a plastic bag. Then
you can toast or defrost slices as you fancy. In my
freezer just now: sliced brioche, mini brioches,
raisin bread, sliced wholemeal bread for packed
lunches, crumpets, croissants, olive bread – the
wherewithal for breakfasts, packed lunches and
teas galore. Simply toast, or microwave for thirty
seconds to defrost and then put in the oven
for a minute. Fabulous.

DON'T WASTE THE CRUSTS

Crusts tend to get wasted or fed to the ducks – which arguably isn't a waste because of the sheer pleasure the children derive from that simple but enjoyable activity (so don't let this tip stop you doing that). But a friend told me she always makes breadcrumbs from her crusts, which strikes me as wonderwoman perfection encapsulated – it allows you to produce things that look like you've put in a lot of effort, when really you've put in very little. Just blitz crusts in the food processor or blender, then freeze the breadcrumbs in a resealable plastic bag or pot. Now you have the instant wherewithal to produce home-made chicken goujons – dip little strips of chicken in beaten egg then roll in breadcrumbs. Or chicken escalopes – just bash out a piece of boneless chicken thigh, add seasoning to the breadcrumbs and cover the chicken. Or simple fish fingers. Or make a posh crust for a piece of fish – squeeze lemon juice over the fish, add chopped herbs and seasoning to the breadcrumbs and press onto the flesh – tasty, chichi, good enough for a dinner party, but practically zero effort. Or mix up the breadcrumbs with some frozen grated cheese and sprinkle over sliced potatoes with a little cream and garlic for a mega-easy and tasty gratin. Bring on the breadcrumbs!

FREEZE GRATED CHEESE

Buy ready-grated packs, or grate your own, stick it in a bag and bung it in the freezer. It will keep for months and you always have grated cheese to hand. If it's clumped together in the bag, just drop it on the floor and the pieces will come apart. No more going to the fridge and finding you don't even have the wherewithal for a toasted cheese sandwich because all the cheese has gone mouldy.

FREEZE BERRIES

Berries never keep long in the fridge, but they will last for months in the freezer. Bung them straight in the freezer in the pack, and you've always got an instant quick, easy and healthy breakfast – just defrost and serve with Greek yogurt. Or whizz them up, straight from frozen, with some almonds and soya milk in the blender for an instant super-healthy and delicious smoothie. Or, blend and add a little icing sugar for a snazzy, but super-easy coulis, to drizzle over shop-bought pudding for an impressive home-made touch.

AND HOW TO DEFROST SOMETHING QUICKLY FROM THE FREEZER

THERE ARE TWO QUICK WAYS OF DEFROSTING QUICKLY (OTHER THAN IN A MICROWAVE):

● Put the item in a sealed bag or container – it must be watertight. Place it in a bowl and fill the bowl with cold water. Berries will defrost this way in seconds, steaks or fish will take minutes and a whole frozen chicken should take about half an hour.

● If you have a griddle with a flat side, you can use it to speed up defrosting. I don't know how it works, but I was told to do this years ago, and it really does work. If you want the item to defrost even quicker, run the griddle under hot water, dry it well and then put the frozen food on it.

★ ★ *Wonder Tip* ★ ★
Put frozen grated cheese on top of home-made pizzas. It takes longer to melt, which means the dough can cook through properly without the cheese getting burned. Pizza perfection!

WHEN YOU'RE COOKING FOR ONE OR TWO, DON'T SCALE DOWN, SCALE UP

How often do you spend ages trying to scale down the quantities in a recipe designed to feed six, when you just want to feed two, or even just you? Instead of faffing with the maths, make the entire quantity and freeze what you don't need in portions – either in plastic tubs or bags. That way, you've got a range of home-made ready meals on tap. If the recipe is just for one or two, it's worth doing a little maths to scale up, so you've got extra to freeze for another day. It's no more work to cook extra, and a lot less than having to start from scratch all over again next time you fancy the same thing. Don't forget to make sure the food has cooled before you freeze it. Batch cooking. I love it.

DISCOVER THE JOY OF SLOW ROASTING

Always on the look out for jobs that do themselves, slow roasting has to be the cooking method of choice when it comes to meat. Basically, you whack whatever it is you're cooking – a joint or a stew – into the oven and cook it low and slow, while you chill out, do other jobs, drink wine, take a bath, whatever you want to do. Cooking meat this way melts the fat away, as it bastes the flesh to produce meltingly tender, falling-apart heavenliness, with no effort on your part at all.

HOW TO KNOW WHEN MEAT OR FISH IS COOKED

To check whether a large piece of meat or fish is cooked through, pierce with a skewer and push it through to the centre. Then hold the skewer to your lips. If it's cold, the meat is not cooked through. If it's warm, the meat's on the rare side. If it's hot, the meat's well cooked. You can tell how well a steak is done by how soft or hard the meat feels. If it feels soft, like a plump marshmallow, when you press into it with a finger, it is rare. The more it cooks through, the firmer the steak gets.

HOW TO STOP MEAT AND FISH STICKING TO THE PAN

The flesh of meat or fish naturally releases from any pan once it's properly seared, so don't try to pull it away from the metal while it's still stuck – you'll just make a mess. Make sure the pan is really hot before the fish or meat goes in, so that it sears the outside, rather than cooking through. Wait until the flesh comes away easily and then flip it over. Sear the second side, and then turn the heat down if you want the flesh to cook through, or alternatively put it in the oven to cook gently.

DON'T FORGET TO LET MEAT REST

Leaving meat to rest makes a massive difference to how tender it will be when you cut into it. Leave steaks for four to five minutes, and a roast for at least ten minutes. Cover it with a tea towel, so that it stays warm.

HOW TO STOP MIX GETTING STUCK ALL OVER YOUR HANDS

When you're making something that requires you to roll up balls of sticky mixture – meatballs, burgers, or anything else – you can stop your hands getting gummed up with the mix by wetting them before you start handling the goo. The water stops the mix from sticking, so you can roll out perfect balls super quickly and with no mess. Just run your hands under the tap periodically to keep them wet. Genius!

TAKE THE HASSLE OUT OF
CLEARING UP AFTER ENTERTAINING

If you've got a dishwasher, always make sure it is completely empty before guests arrive (even if it means doing half a load to clear it), so that you can just throw all the pans, dirty plates, glasses, cutlery and anything else straight in once everyone has gone. It makes clearing up a cinch. Simply turn on the machine and you'll wake up to a clean kitchen. So much nicer than having to face congealing plates in the morning. Euw.

Wonder Tip

Reduce smoke by pan frying in grapeseed oil, which has a high smoking point, and rub oil over the meat or fish, rather than pouring it in the pan.

HOW TO GET THE SHARPEST
KNIVES YOU'VE EVER HAD

Having sharp knives is important because they make your life so much easier. Trying to cut anything with a blunt knife becomes a total chore. My first cheeky tip on this front is to forget trying to sharpen the blades yourself – take them to the butcher. In exchange for some gratitude and a box of chocolates or tip in the charity box, a good local butcher should be more than happy to help. Learning how to sharpen knives

is a skill that takes butchers years to hone, so having a crack at it yourself with a knife stone or steel will, more likely than not, leave you with even blunter knives than before. The butcher's skill will give you the sharpest knives you've ever had, which make slicing anything a cinch. The next trick is...

...HOW TO KEEP KNIVES SHARP

Never put knives in the dishwasher, as it will blunt them. Always clean the knife as soon as you have used it, before anything hardens onto the blade. Just run under the hot tap, spritz a little washing-up liquid on a brush and scrub. Dry immediately and put away, either in a wooden block, or in a protective sleeve. Never use a hard chopping board – wood or plastic are best.

The
LAUNDRY

Unfortunately there is no way round it. It's boring. Every day feels like groundhog day as you wonder how the pile of clothes got so big. Short of making everyone go round in dirty clothes, there aren't many shortcuts with the washing itself. (Luckily it's another story come the drying tips in a moment). First, a couple of washing tips. Pile everything on the floor together and sort into manageable piles of items that can be washed together. Always remember a rash decision to bundle things together for the sake of ease, even though you know the colours might run or that something might shrink, might come back to haunt you when favourite clothes have been ruined – or at least aren't quite how they should be. Always check the front of clothes and (with children's especially) the cuffs. Spray a stain remover on any marks before they go into the machine. You really don't want to have to double the effort by rewashing anything that doesn't get clean first time around.

SAVE A FORTUNE ON LAUNDRY PRODUCTS
Using soda crystals on your laundry will save you a small fortune buying ridiculously expensive pots of specialised cleaning powders to add to the wash to get clothes ultra clean. Seriously, soda crystals work just as well – and they cost about ten times less. In addition to boosting the power of your washing powder, the soda crystals work to clean the machine itself by dissolving the grease and residue which can block pipes. So two jobs for the price of one – nice. All you need to do is add about 2 tablespoons in with the washing powder for a large load, 1 tablespoon for a medium load and ½ tablespoon for a small one.

MAKE YOUR OWN STAIN-REMOVING SPRAY
Another product that I used to spend a fortune on was stain-removing spray. They do work brilliantly but are so expensive. So when I finished a spray, I tried mixing 400ml white vinegar and 2 teaspoons on bicarbonate of soda in a large bowl. You need to stir vigorously until it stops fizzing, then pour it into a jug and decant into a spray bottle. I decided that if it didn't work as well as the sprays I would start buying them again, as I worried that it might be a false economy if clothes started getting ruined by permanent stains that my new cheap cleaner wouldn't remove. I have never switched back. On occasion I have had to wash something twice – but that also used to happen before. Always shake the bottle well to mix up the solution before using.

This works really well on upholstery and carpet stains too. Don't forget it's the job of manufacturers to make us think we need specific products for each job. They want to make money – we want to save it to spend on something much more fun!

STAIN REMOVER FOR WHITES
To give extra cleaning power on whites, add some lemon juice to the stain-removing spray – lemon is a natural bleach. Place a muslin or tea-towel over a jug and strain the liquid over it, to remove any pith that might block the spray. For really tough stains, sprinkle bicarbonate of soda on the stain and spray white vinegar over it so that it fizzes up. Leave for half an hour then wash as normal. It's best not to use this on coloured fabrics.

This is where the fabulous soda crystals come into their own – they are bargainously cheap and they work miraculously.

Get rid of smells under the arms of clothes

It's so annoying when washing doesn't seem to freshen the armpits of certain items of clothing where the fabric seems almost impregnated with the whiff of stale body odour under the arms. You've gone to all the effort of cleaning and drying it and as soon as the heat of the iron comes into contact with it, the smell returns - so frustrating. An effective way of solving the problem is to spray the area of fabric with white vinegar before laundering. Phew.

Home-made laundry softener

Please don't switch off at this point. I know it sounds like a case of 'life's too short', but seriously you should try this. I made some one day when I had run out of the super-expensive softener I was having to buy because one of my daughters was allergic to everything else. I didn't have time to go and buy more, and I had a massive pile of washing. I figured I'd give making some a go and I was genuinely surprised by how worth doing it was. For starters, it takes about two seconds to make. Secondly, it works brilliantly. Thirdly, my daughter is not allergic to it. Fourthly, it is so cheap to make. Fifthly, I won't ever run out of softener again because I can just make more. So here's how to do it (for half a litre):

- **300ml white vinegar**
- **30 drops lavender oil**
- **200ml water**

Make it up in a measuring jug. You'll need to do it twice to fill a litre bottle. First pour in the vinegar. Add the lavender oil and water. Stir and pour into your bottle. If you have a label maker, stamp out one with 'softener' on it, so it looks stylish too. Shake well before each use.

Make your own scented ironing water

Spraying clothes with water to dampen them slightly makes ironing much easier, and you it's really nice to scent the clothes at the same time. Just fill a spray bottle with water and spritz in some squirts of your favourite perfume. Add twenty, sniff, and if it's not strong enough, add a few more. It's a great way to use those little free samples perfume counters give away. Fabulously smelling clothes for freeeee.

Stop having to iron your laundry

Well... most of it anyway. You can save yourself loads of time and effort (and money if you're paying someone else to iron for you) by whittling down what has to be ironed to a tiny fraction of what comes out of the drier, without everything ending up looking crumpled and scruffy. Firstly, when you are loading the drier give a good shake to anything that's emerged twisted from the final spin in the wash, so that it is flat when it goes into the machine. Once it's dried, the trick is to spend a little bit of time folding and smoothing when you unload the machine. If you can, unload the drier as soon as it's finished because if you fold the clothes while they're still warm, creases won't have had a chance to set in. Smooth out and press firmly as you fold. If there are big items, shake them out vigorously before folding. If you're not able to unload while the clothes are still warm, don't worry – just make sure the door isn't opened before you are ready to fold because the cold air will fix creases into the fabric. Stack everything into a large plastic trug, so you can carry the folded pile around easily – and the weight of the clothes on top of each other keeps them smooth.

Do the ironing twice as fast

A few tips to make the ironing quicker, easier, and dare I say it, maybe even enjoyable! One of the most basic ways to help you speed through a mountain of ironing is to deploy the biggest, widest ironing board you can find. It's obvious really – with each swoosh of the iron you can cover a larger area before having to reposition the item. It makes ironing sheets, so much easier. Secondly, buy the best steam iron you can afford. Used with ironing water, pressing even the most crumpled clothes and sheets will be a breeze.

Also, no matter how much of a hurry you are in, never put the iron straight onto an item of clothing the moment it's got hot. I have lost count of the number of times I've raced into ironing something I need urgently, only for the iron to sputter out dirty water all over the item – invariably something white. Disaster, and more work created. Instead, go over a tea-towel a few times with the steam on to get rid of any mineral deposits lurking in the water tank. If the base plate is dirty, clean it before turning on the iron by spritzing white vinegar over and buffing it up with a damp microfibre cloth.

Of course the best way to cut ironing time, is to cut the number of clothes that need to be pressed. We've already talked about how to press most items with your hands so they don't need to be ironed. Avoid buying clothes that need ironing, if there's a good alternative. For instance kids pyjamas. Those gorgeous little cotton pyjamas might look adorable, but you won't appreciate them so much every time you find yourself labouring over them with a hot iron to get rid of the creases. Instead buy pyjamas in stretchy t-shirt fabric that can be pressed flat by hand. And if you can find easy-iron shirts that don't look like they're going to stick to the nearest balloon because they're so static with nylon, go for those, too.

★ Wonder Tip

A wall-mounted airer is ingenious (and I would say vital) for air-drying clothes if you don't want stuff hanging over every radiator. They fold pretty flat against the wall, but you can always hang one on the back of a door if you don't have space, or don't want it in sight – although I think the wooden ones look pretty stylish. The beauty of the wall-mounted option is that they don't take up floor space like a free-standing drier. Try to order the washing loads so that you don't have a massive pile of stuff to try to fit on the airer all at once. You can use it to hang clothes to dry on hangers too. Smooth everything first to make the ironing as painless as possible.

Always give the drum a good spin
between loads to double-check
nothing has been left inside
that might ruin the next wash.

THE ART OF MACHINE MAINTENANCE

WASHING MACHINE

A broken-down washing machine in a busy household is a nightmare. I'm sure we've all been there. What a hassle. It always takes so long for the repair guy to come – meanwhile the washing is piling up and you're schlepping to the launderette spending even more time you don't have on the dullest task of all. So it's worth spending a little bit of effort to try and avoid a breakdown. Here are some tips I elicited from a great washing machine repair guy I came across. He says the main cause of breakdown is a blockage in the pipes.

- Always check all pockets for coins, hairclips, stones – anything that might cause a problem. Bra wires are a big problem too apparently, so check there are no holes they might escape through before washing. (I know, you're not supposed to machine wash them, but really, who doesn't?)
- Pipes also get blocked by grease and detergent residue, so once a month put half a pack of soda crystals (i.e. 500g) in the tub of the machine and do a boil wash cycle.
- Regularly clean out the detergent drawer to stop build-up. It should pull out easily so you can rinse it in the sink.
- Never overload the machine. When you've got a massive mountain of washing it's tempting to get through it as quickly as possible by filling the drum to the max. The problem is that once the water comes swooshing in it will put too much weight in the drum and stress on the mechanisms. Eventually something will give out. And anyway the clothes don't get cleaned properly that way – they need space to swirl around freely rather than being clumped together.

TUMBLE DRIER

Again, prevention is better than cure. And again, blockages and overloading are the main reasons for breakdown.

- Clean the fluff filters every time you use the machine. Hopefully you're lucky and your machine has one that is simple to slide in and out of the door. If it's not obvious how to do it, check the manual or phone the manufacturer for guidance. If you see a build-up of fluff anywhere that you can't remove by hand easily, vacuum it.
- If your machine vents to the outside, check the vent on the outside wall periodically to make sure it is clear. Vacuum around the vent on full power to remove any fluff or debris that might block it.
- If you have a condenser dryer, clean the heat exchanger at least four times a year – it's the big block of layered corrugated metal that pulls out at the bottom of the machine. It is a hassle to clean it, but if you don't and too much fluff builds up, the thermostat on the machine can blow, which is an even bigger pain. Clean it by vacuuming or leaving to sit in warm water for twenty minutes or so, then shaking well to knock out fluff that's accumulated between the fragile layers of metal.
- If you have a condenser dryer, empty out the water reservoir every time you use the machine. The machine will automatically switch off when the reservoir is full, which can be a total pain if you've left a load on to dry and only realise it's switched itself off when you go to remove the washing.
- Don't overload. It strains the mechanics of the machine – and anyway, the clothes will bunch together too much, which means they'll dry creased.

The
BEDROOM

ALWAYS MAKE THE BED

The idea of making the bed is always worse than actually doing it – which really does only take seconds. Always make sure it's done before you leave the house, because coming home to unmade beds is just depressing. Going to bed in crumpled sheets, ditto. If you make a bed properly, getting into it at night is comforting and soothing. Think how lovely it feels when you slide under the crisp sheets of a freshly made bed. A very simple pleasure.

So here's how to achieve that in seconds every morning. Beds do need to air a little before being made, so when you get up, pull the covers right back and open the window a little to get fresh air into the room. By the time you've showered and had breakfast they'll be fine to make up again. Shake out or plump up the pillows and give the duvet a good airing by holding the bottom corners and shaking out. Pull the sheet tight across the mattress and tuck in well – any creases will automatically disappear. Tuck the bottom of the duvet in between the mattress and the bed frame and it will be easy to stretch out and smooth. Do this before pillows – whether you put them underneath the duvet or on top – as that way the duvet will lie properly flat and hotel smooth.

HOW TO CHANGE A DUVET COVER

Changing bedding can be exhausting work as you grapple with getting the duvet into its cover, practically crawling inside to make sure the corners all meet up. There is a much more dignified and simple way of getting the job done in a flash. Lay the empty duvet as it should be on the bed. Get the clean cover and turn it inside out. Ruche the cover up over your arms so that your hands can hold the top two corners of the cover from the inside. Now stand at the foot of the bed and lean forward to grab the top two corners of the duvet. Hold onto them tightly through the cover, so the top two corners are clenched in your fists, and then yank your arms towards you. As you do that the duvet will miraculously come through with cover smoothly on, corners in place. Make sure the bottom corners of duvet and cover are together and give a good shake from the bottom. Simple, no sweat.

DON'T STRESS ABOUT CHANGING BEDDING IN THE NIGHT IF A CHILD'S BEEN SICK OR WET THE BED

Keep sleeping bags in the cupboard with the bedding for a no-hassle night-time bedding swap. Don't even think about trying to put fresh sheets on when you're groggy with sleep and desperate to crawl back to bed.

> ★ **Wonder Tip**
> Keep your laundry cupboard organised by sticking labels onto the edges of shelves to identify bedding for different sized beds.

Plump up pillows and cushions to the max, and kill off dust mites by blasting them in the tumble dryer.

DECLUTTER YOUR WARDROBE

One of the main problem areas in a bedroom is an over-crammed wardrobe. Squeezing clothes into a jammed wardrobe becomes arduous, so you end up piling things on a chair, or the floor. Keep your wardrobe clear and so many benefits will flow from that. At a basic level, it's easier to keep your room tidy, but more fundamentally, it will make you feel better about yourself. You know what's in the wardrobe, so it's easier to find something to wear. And by getting rid of the stuff you never wear, you eliminate the guilt of being reminded every day of purchases that were actually a total waste of money.

How many items are pieces that you're hanging onto because they were expensive or they've got a good label, when actually you never feel that great in them because maybe your shape has changed since you bought them, or the colour or fit just isn't quite you, or it was a sale piece that you only really bought because it was cheap? Well it's time for the mother of all clear-outs. And you know what will make it all worthwhile? You can sell your cast-offs to raise money for replacements! So here are some tips for how to have a good wardrobe purge:

- Focus on one area at a time, i.e. a shelf or a hanging rail, and pull everything out of that section.
- Be ruthless. Go through each item with a critical eye. Assess how often you wear it and how it makes you feel. Try things on and take a good rear-view look if you can, either using strategically placed full-length mirrors, or a hand-held mirror and a full-length one.
- The first group of things to get rid of is easy – anything you've not worn for at least a year. There's most likely a reason you haven't worn it, unless it genuinely is something you'd forgotten you even had.
- Regard good labels as currency. If you're planning a big sell-off online a well-known label will attract buyers to your collection of cast-offs, so don't hang onto something just because of the label.
- Try to scrutinise yourself from all angles in the mirror. Looking at a reflection in a reflection, rather than directly into the mirror, lets you see things more objectively, helping you to assess whether something suits you or not.
- Remember the rear view is just as important. You might not see it normally. It doesn't mean everyone else doesn't.
- Remind yourself of the number of times you have declared, 'I have nothing to wear'. Unless your wardrobe is completely empty, that's patently not true. It's just that what's in there isn't fitting the bill, so bear in mind what you actually need clothes for when going through them.
- We all have a wardrobe staple that we seem to gravitate to buying again and again – maybe a white shirt or black trousers. Infinitely useful of course, but unless it's your daily uniform and you never wear anything else, you've probably got far more than you need. Weed out the ones that don't flatter or fit properly.
- Make a list of what you need and stick it in your bag so you've got it to hand next time you go shopping.

Wonder Tip

Keep a bag of pegs in your wardrobe to stop clothes slipping off hangers. (See page 133 for how to transform free metal hangers into ultra-stylish hangers worthy of a funky boutique in seconds.)

Transform a badly fitting jacket from frumpy to fabulous with a brooch

When you're going through your clothes deciding what to keep and what to ditch, don't discount a jacket just because it doesn't fit you properly anymore. Anything can be transformed with an instant tailoring job using a brooch. If it's too big, pull it tight around you and secure with the brooch for a chic tailored look. If it's too tight, forget the buttons and pin it together with the brooch instead. You want it to look like a deliberate style statement, so remove the buttons and pin the brooch strategically, either right in the centre, or towards the top. You can buy really beautiful old paste brooches quite cheaply at antique and flea markets. Start collecting!

Wonder Tip

A brooch is a great quick fix if you pull something out to wear and realise it's lost a button. Keep a jar of badges for the same trick with kids clothes.

Store out-of-season clothes somewhere else

Obviously most items get worn year round, but to avoid clutter, you don't want something that's not being worn taking up valuable wardrobe space. So wash, fold and store summer clothes in winter, and vice versa.

Repair and wear

If you've got something you're not wearing just because it needs a repair or adjustment, sort it. It's a waste of space otherwise.

Wardrobe tip

Keep a small roll of double-sided tape and a pair of scissors in your wardrobe to use for emergency repairs and to make sure clothes stay where they should. It's so annoying when you pull a skirt or trousers out to wear in a hurry and realise the hem's coming down – just hold it with a bit of double-sided tape until you've got time to do a proper fix. And it does the same trick as the expensive 'tit tape' that stars use for the red carpet to make sure their dresses don't gape and expose too much flesh (well sometimes, anyway) – just use a little bit if you want to be sure something stays put.

How to get your fashion mojo

A good way of helping to define your style is to choose a fashion soulmate, someone who encapsulates a look you really like and whose style would work for you. In other words, if you want a casual daytime look, don't choose a celebrity who is only ever pictured at red carpet events. Have her in mind for your uber-glam vibe if you want, but choose someone more homely for the practical stuff. It's not about copying someone, but about being able to visualise subjectively, which is very difficult to do when you're standing in front of a mirror. If you're not sure about an item of clothing, try to picture it on your style icon. It helps you make an objective assessment. So when you're shopping and are feeling adventurous and veering towards something wacky or utterly different to what you'd normally go for, think: 'Would that look fresh and fabulous on my fashion soulmate, or slightly ridiculous?'

Are you tempted by something just because it's a bargain or it's cheap? It won't be a bargain if you end up never wearing it. Don't forget the price becomes irrelevant when you're wearing the item in terms of how it makes you feel – either it suits you and makes you feel good, or it doesn't. Something cheap can look expensive and vice versa.

Unless you're absolutely sure about something, don't buy it. Always try things on again at home. Sometimes something that looked great in the shop suddenly doesn't look as fabulous when you get home – whether it's the mirrors, the lighting, whatever. If you change your mind once you're home, put it straight back in the bag, with the receipt and leave it by the door so you don't forget to take it back ASAP.

Restore a bobbly jumper

It's so annoying when a nice jumper – or anything else woollen – goes bobbly and looks scruffy as a result. The quickest and easiest route to bobble-free beauty is to give it a good groom with a nit comb. Yes, I do mean one of those combs normally used to trawl for nits in a child's hair! Much better than one of those electronic gadgets, which take forever and don't actually work very well at all. All you need to do is lay the nit comb fairly flat against the item to be de-bobbled and slide it over the surface, snagging the bobbles in the teeth as you go. Be careful not to snag and pull stitches as you go. Probably the most enjoyable thing you'll ever do with a nit comb.

General

SAVE A FORTUNE BY NOT HAVING TO REPAINT YOUR WALLS AND WOODWORK

Here is a genius ruse to make it look as though everything's been freshly painted – when in fact all it needed was a good clean. When you've got children, pen marks, scuffs, handprints and general grime quickly accrue on surfaces, making everything look and feel a bit dingy. Think of this as a brilliant money-saving tip, because once you've cleaned all of that off, the walls and woodwork will look as though they've been repainted, with very little effort and zero expense. All you need are two damp cloths and some scouring cream. Use one cloth to apply the cream and to rub away the dirty marks. Wipe over with the clean damp cloth so that no powdery residue is left once it dries. Don't worry about making patches on the walls – as long as you wipe over properly with the clean cloth the wall will dry evenly. (Keep rinsing out the clean cloth so that it stays clean.)

CLEAN BRASS IN AN INSTANT

Cleaning brass with traditional cleaners is one of the messiest jobs you can do. Well, here is a fabulous way to restore the shine to top bling condition, without blackening your nails in the process! Squeeze the juice from half a lemon. Add a teaspoon of bicarbonate of soda. It will froth like crazy. Get a cloth and rub it over the brass. It works instantly. I mean instantly! No elbow grease required. Rub it gently all over and clean off. To get a long-lasting shine, go over with furniture polish. Buff up with a microfibre cloth and admire.

SAVE HAVING TO CLEAN SOFA COVERS

The arms of sofas and upholstered chairs are the first places to get grubby and look scruffy. A great way to protect them is to fold up blankets and drape them over the arms. It looks stylish and it's practical and cosy too, because you've always got extra warmth to hand on a chilly evening. And it's so much easier to sling the blankets in the wash rather than having to clean the entire sofa cover.

Cut out the laborious task of sewing name tags into children's clothes

Never waste any time sewing name tags into children's clothes. Just get an indelible fabric pen and write their names straight onto the label. Job done in about a second. I know the beautiful, old-fashioned, embroidered version is so pleasing and lovely to admire in your child's school uniform, but seriously, why would you want to create an extra job for yourself?

How to clean radiators super easily

Cleaning radiators is one of those horribly fiddly tasks that probably never gets done because it's difficult, and anyway it's easy to ignore. Until something falls behind the radiator and then you realise how gross it is. Apart from anything else, the accumulated dust and fluff is a haven for dust mites galore. So it's worth buying a radiator brush – you can get them very cheaply. They are long and wriggly, like a fluffed-up snake, so they get into the teeniest gaps. They are actually really satisfying to use. They're also very handy for fishing things out when they get knocked and stuck behind the radiator. Use this super -handy gadget to clean any hard-to-reach spot.

Use baby oil to nourish and shine

A wipe with a little baby oil is a brilliant and quick way to get stainless steel and slate looking like new. Use sparingly so that it rubs in well – too much and it will just be a dust magnet. Do this on outdoor furniture too, to protect it over winter.

Clean windows in seconds

...and for free! All you need is a trusty microfibre cloth and a damp disposable cloth – no need for any detergent or sprays. Wipe over first with the damp cloth, then rub well with the microfibre to remove any smears. Really, that's it. It couldn't be easier or quicker.

Ban any non-washable children's pens and paints

Only ever buy washable felt-tips and other art stuff when you've got little ones. If kids are given something that isn't washable, hide it away until they're bigger, or pass it on to someone else. You can't stop small children getting pen on their clothes – and probably the walls and other surfaces too. At least if it's washable you know it will come off easily.

The
FULL CLEAN

As with everything, little and often is the right approach when facing a whole house that needs a full spring clean. Actually I would say the term 'spring clean' is misleading. It's the tail end of winter, when the sun is low and shines beautifully but unforgivingly through dirty windows, highlighting the dust and dirt that has gathered during the darkest months unnoticed. Break the task into bite-sized chunks and just focus on one room at a time. Here is my guide on how to blitz a room and get the sparkle back in, with least effort and maximum results:

START AT THE TOP AND WORK DOWN.

● Get a long-handled duster (if you don't have one, wrap a microfibre cloth around the bristles of a broom) and sweep along the top of walls and around cornices (if you have them), to get rid of dust or cobwebs.

● Get the vacuum cleaner and set the suction to low, because you are going to use it on textiles and it's really frustrating when they just keep getting sucked right up into the cleaner. Go over curtains, the tops of doors, sofas, chairs, cushions, lampshades and skirting boards, pulling out the furniture to make sure you get rid of all the fluff and dust that is lurking behind.

● Get a damp cloth and a dry microfibre cloth. Take everything off all surfaces (but only do one area at a time) and wipe over with the damp cloth to clean away the dust. Rinse out the cloth and repeat as often as you need to be sure the surface is clean. Buff dry with the microfibre cloth.

● Do the same to all objects before they go back. Note: There is no need to use cleaning products. The combination of wet wipe and dry microfibre cleans and shines everything – including silver picture frames.

● Do the same for mirrors and picture glass, the TV and computer screens. Lastly, clean the windows. Again, no need for any cleaning products. It is important though to keep rinsing your cleaning cloth – or replace it, if it gets too dirty or ragged. Likewise, have a spare microfibre to hand if the one you are using gets too damp.

● Clean off any stubborn marks on paintwork with a little scouring cream and wash away thoroughly with a clean damp cloth. Almost done.

● All you need to do now is vacuum the floor. If you have rugs, take them outside and give them a good shake. If you have hard floors, hoover or sweep and clean. (See page 35 for how to clean floors.)

● If you have carpet, use a cleaning spray on any dirty marks and then hoover on full suction power.

★ Wonder Tip

If you move a piece of furniture while cleaning and indentations have been left behind on a rug or carpet, you can use an ice cube to restore the pile. Just put the cube over the mark and leave it to melt for a while. The fibres of the rug or carpet will absorb the water and swell up. If it's a carpet, gently scratch your nail over the crushed fibres to help separate them out, so that they bounce back to their original position. If it's a rug, lift it and push the fibres up from underneath.

Pest

CONTROL

MOTHS

Quite possibly one of the most irritating pests known to womankind because of their incredible ability to destroy favourite items of clothing right under our noses. Annoyingly they have discerning tastes and will always go for natural fibres – probably the finest things in your wardrobe – so if you've got moths, it can be an expensive problem. Getting to grips with them is a little time-consuming, but not impossible. First know your enemy. If you can see any of those tiny, papery, golden moths flitting about kamikaze fashion, they've probably already wreaked some destruction. The process begins when a pregnant female finds her way into the dark cosy depths of your wardrobe and lays her miniscule eggs between the fibres and hairs of your clothes. As the larvae develop they will eat away at the fabric, which has now become their food supply. Finally they pop out as moths, mate with each other, lay more eggs on

your clothes, and so on. So here's what you need to do to stop them in their tracks:

● If you think you've got a problem, empty your wardrobe, then use the vacuum cleaner on full power to suction away every single bit of dust and fluff. Wipe lavender oil (a natural moth repellant) over all the surfaces of the wardrobe.

● Check over every item of clothing before you put it back. If anything has tell-tale holes, keep it out. Don't put any woollens away either. Also keep out anything that is especially precious, even if there are no signs yet of any holes. At this stage, you could actually wash or dry clean every item to be sure the problem is completely clear, but as that would be super expensive and time-consuming, pick your battles for now.

● Dry cleaning, washing in high temperatures and freezing will destroy moth eggs, so either hot wash the clothes (if possible), send to be dry cleaned, or wrap in a plastic bag and put in the freezer for three days.

- Lay pheromone traps in the wardrobe. These are little cardboard boxes lined with a sticky surface impregnated with pheromones. Male moths will be attracted to it and then can't escape. If they can't get the females pregnant, you've stopped the cycle.
- Check other areas that might be harbouring moths in the bedroom, such as a sofa, the carpet, under the bed and drawers – signs are dead moths and silvery threads. Vacuum and clean well. Put a pheromone trap inside or under the furniture.

TO STOP MOTHS COMING BACK

- Moths will be lured to an item of clothing if it's got protein, i.e. food splatters, on it, so don't be tempted to put dirty clothes away. (Sounds gross when put like that, but we probably all do it.)
- Protect precious clothes with zippable bags and cases, which you can buy from specialist storage companies. They aren't cheap, but will protect your clothes forever.
- Protect wool and coats from moths by putting loose lavender in the pockets
- Replace the pheromone traps every few months. stowed inside to ward off destructive moths – it seems to have worked.

MICE

Mice are everywhere and are always on the lookout for a cosy gaff with readily available tidbits, so the most obvious way of avoiding them – or indeed any other pests like ants or cockroaches – is not to leave food hanging around, and always sweep up any bits that fall on the floor. If you can't face completely clearing up the kitchen before bed every night,

at the very least always put all leftovers away, or scrape them into the bin, and put all dirty plates, pans and bowls in the sink soaking. Pest issues aside, it's so much nicer to come down to a clean kitchen the next morning. If mice are already in, before you unleash the traps or go to the expense of calling in pest control, try sprinkling paprika around the areas where the mice are likely to be coming in. Check everywhere for mouse droppings – under work surfaces, around the fridge, behind furniture, etc – for evidence of mouse poos. Hoover them all away, then sprinkle a light dusting of paprika in those places. One sniff and the mice should run away and try to find somewhere else a little more accommodating.

WOODWORM

Always check old furniture for signs of woodworm before bringing it into the house. The obvious sign is the little telltale holes, but they only mean that a piece has had woodworm. The holes are caused when the adult beetles have hatched and emerged from the wood to take flight. The beetle larvae can be burrowed in the wood munching away unnoticed for several years before that happens. To check if the woodworm is still active, knock around the holes. If fine wood dust comes out, it probably is. It's actually very easy to treat an individual piece of furniture, although if there are loads of holes, it might take a while! Basically you need to buy special fluid from the hardware store. It comes in a container with a pointy nozzle. Inject the liquid into all the holes, via the nozzle. If the furniture has a waxed finish you can also buy special treatment wax, which will fill the holes and kill woodworm.

Doing it
YOURSELF

NOW I'M NOT TRYING to pile on the pressure by saying

that women should do absolutely everything around the

house. However, I would say that it is empowering to be

able to do DIY. Maybe I'm odd, but I actually love doing

it, because it's so satisfying to get a great result from

something you have done yourself.

DIY
AND PAINTING

This is a prime area where you want to save money on the boring stuff, so that you can spend it on the fun stuff. This isn't intended to be a complete guide to DIY – there are entire manuals if that's what you're after. This is the cherry-picked wonderwoman's guide, i.e., a fairly narrow repertoire of things that are easy to do, and will make a difference to your life.

WHAT YOU NEED IN YOUR TOOLBOX:
- **Drill with attachments** A very basic drill should do.
- **Range of screwdrivers** Two flat head and two Philips (for screws with a cross-head) should cover most jobs – one small and one large.
- **Hammer**
- **Bradawl** A small super-useful tool that you use to bore holes into walls, wood, tin cans – anything.
- **Wallplugs and screws** A selection of sizes.
- **Spirit level**

- **Extension leads** I prefer to use a short extension lead with multi-sockets, rather than a multi-socket adaptor directly into the wall, because you can trail it away and conceal it behind furniture, curtains, whatever, to hide messy cables and plugs. Also, keep at least one extra long one for lengthening cables when necessary.
- **Radiator keys** For bleeding radiators (see page 79).
- **Pliers** Always useful.
- **Adjustable wrench** Ditto.
- **A couple of filling knives** One wide, one narrow.
- **Cable detector**
- **Tape measure**
- **Masking tape**

Not for the toolbox, but handy to keep nearby: stocks of batteries and light bulbs – so you've always got spares to hand.

A well-stocked tool box is a curiously satisfying thing. It doesn't have to be a proper builder's type box. A basket or something more stylish works just as well, and is much more pleasing to look at on a shelf.

How to paint

Painting is very easy and very satisfying. It is one of the easiest and cheapest ways you can transform a room. With a little bit of know-how and effort you can deliver just as good a job as a professional. To keep builder's costs down, if I am having work done I will always do the painting myself – cupboards, shelves, walls, ceilings (this one took a while for me to crack and be confident with, but really it's okay), skirting boards, doors – and I genuinely enjoy doing it. I have to admit the worst part can sometimes be geeing myself up to begin, but once I'm going I remember how easy it is – and how glad I am not to be paying someone else to do it. For the most professional and uniform finish always use a roller. And happily that is also the quickest and easiest way to paint. Here's what you need to get going:

- **Paint** (of course) – as a general rule, emulsion for walls, eggshell or gloss for woodwork
- **Roller frame** – use a mini roller (called a radiator or 'rad' roller) for a small job, and a large one for walls
- **Roller sleeve,** which slides onto the frame. Smooth is best for gloss/eggshell and lambswool for emulsion.
- **8cm nylon brush**
- **Paint tray**
- **Baby wipes**
- **Sandpaper**
- **Clingfilm**
- **Something to protect the floor,** or any other surfaces you don't want to get paint on
- **Masking tape**
- **Blocks**
- **A shower cap** (to protect your hair, especially if you're painting a ceiling)

If you've never painted before that might seem like a long, slightly daunting list. Stay with me –once you're equipped and started you will never look back.

Starting from scratch

If you are going to decorate from scratch, the job requires a bit more effort, so here's the blow-by-blow guide, starting with filling. Filling holes and cracks in walls is really easy if you buy the right stuff.

TO FILL A HOLE OR CRACK IN THE WALL

You can buy tubs of ready-mixed filler that feel like there is nothing in them because they are so light. That is the stuff you want for holes and cracks. It is very easy to use, dries quickly, can be sanded down and painted over and stores really well. One pot will probably last you forever. First of all, if necessary, hoover away any dust from the hole. Put a relatively small-sized blob of filler on a filling knife and squish it into the hole by putting the blade at a 45-degree angle to the wall (filler side down obviously), and scrape it over the area to be filled. Add more filler to the blade if necessary and repeat. The filler will sink into the hole as it dries, so you want to pack it as solidly into the area as possible. Scrape the blade over the area, always at a 45-degree angle, to remove excess filler and to smooth. For a crack, just drag the blade the length of it. Before painting over, lightly sand with a fine grade sandpaper, to make sure the area is smooth. It might look smooth, but any scrape marks or bumps will show once it's painted, so feel with your hand for smoothness and sand if necessary.

TO FILL CRACKS AROUND WINDOWS AND DOORS

Again, no skill required, just a little know-how. For these areas, you need to use a flexible filler – decorator's caulk. You will also need a caulk gun and a packet of baby wet wipes. First of all, unscrew the nozzle of the caulk tube and cut off the moulded tip of the container so that the filler can be dispensed. Screw the pointy nozzle back on and cut off the tip for the caulk to flow through. The hole should match the size of the gap you're filling. For a thin crack, just cut off the very tip of the hole (although the hole should not be so small that it is too hard to squeeze out). For a thicker crack cut a slightly longer bit off. Put the canister in the gun and hold the lever so that the disc that pushes into the tube slides down to lock it firmly in place. To release the filler just squeeze the trigger. Squeeze caulk along the full length of the crack. Don't stress about making a dead straight line, or if there's too much filler, or little gaps in the line. Put a baby wipe over the tip of your forefinger abd smooth along the caulk, wiping away the excess as you go. Smooooth.

Don't be too precious about
        taking down blinds and
curtains - just paint
        carefully around them.

TOUCHING UP WALLS

It's so quick and easy to touch up walls, for a really satisfying result. As long as you have a flat (i.e. no-shine) emulsion on the walls and are using exactly the same colour (from the original tin is best if possible), the areas you touch up should blend seamlessly into the rest.

For this reason, always go for flat paint when decorating walls. Forget finishes that are supposedly easy to clean. You can wipe flat paint surfaces to clean off marks (see page 60) just as easily – and if you need to retouch you can. Other types of paint might look patchy where you touch up. It doesn't mean you can't do it, but you might need to repaint a much larger area (i.e. between defined points), so it doesn't look messy. Always stir the paint really well before using so that the colour is properly blended. If you are just touching up a really small area, you can use a brush. No need for a paint tray, just dip it straight in the pot. Scrape gently against the sides of the tin to remove excess paint and brush gently over the area. Build up thin layers if necessary to avoid brushstrokes, and feather the paint away from the area you're retouching. If you are covering a larger area, use a roller.

Before you put your roller in the paint, make sure there are no loose fibres, which will stick straight to the painted surface, giving an annoying hairy effect.

Get rid of any by going over the roller with some sticky tape, as if you're waxing it.

Put the roller in the paint, scrape it over the ridged part of the tray as you bring it out, and roll away. You want the roller to have enough paint so that it glides on smoothly, but not so much that it spatters everywhere. If you're not sure how much you need, it's always best to start with less and add more. That's it. You're up and running. Now no job is beyond your reach. Go girl!

OK, the joy is in the painting. The tedious part is in the cleaning up. But there are ways of making light work of that. You've already neatly avoided one job by lining the tray with clingfilm. Cleaning any water-based paint off a brush is really easy – just run it under the tap,

If you've started a job and don't have time to finish it, you can keep paint on a brush or roller for several days, with the help of some clingfilm. Just wrap really well and the paint will stay wet for about five days.

Now for a slightly controversial suggestion. I know the mantra on everything is to recycle and reuse – and I really do try to do that with most things – but for me, I'm afraid, cleaning oil-based paints off a brush falls into the 'life is too short' category, so my solution is to just bin it. Argh. I know it's wasteful, but I can tell you I've shared my dirty little secret with fellow DIYers – and I am not alone. They agree the dread of the tedious cleaning at the end can be enough to put you off doing the job in the first place so being a little wasteful in order to make sure the job is done is a just one. If you're desperate to be a paragon of virtue here, leave the brush soaking in white spirits in a glass jar before washing it out.

Wonder Tip

Before pouring paint into the tray, line it with clingfilm. When you're done just pull away the clingfilm and you have a clean tray ready to use again. Lush.

TO PAINT A WALL

First of all, make sure all holes and cracks are filled. Rub your hand over the wall to check it is completely smooth. Sand gently if necessary. Hoover away any dust on top of the skirting board. Line the paint tray with clingfilm, then pour in paint so the well is a maximum two-thirds full. Dip an 8cm brush in the paint and squeeze it against the tray to remove excess.

First you need to paint around the edges to get a clean line between the wall and ceiling, the wall and base, and anything else, like a window, so that when you roller the walls you are colouring in between the lines. Angle the brush at 45 degrees from the wall and just allow the tips of the bristles to touch. Now switch the angle of the brush so that it is 45 degrees from the wall in the direction you are going to drag it to make your line. This will corral the bristles into a point – you want to draw the line right along the edge, without touching the ceiling, skirting, etc. The beauty of doing this is it saves you all the time and effort of masking up. If you do get some paint where you don't want it, just grab a wet wipe and rub it away. Once the edges are done, the rest is simple. Use a large roller and you can get it done pretty quickly. To get a smooth, even finish, press the roller gently against the wall. Whenever you're painting, keep an eye out for drips and smooth over them before they set.

Wonder Tip

Before using a brush, always make sure there are no loose hairs that will stick to the wall. Hold the handle firmly in one hand and swish the bristles vigorously back and forth with the other to make any loose hairs come out.

TO BLOCK OUT A STAIN

If there is a stain on the wall that won't be covered by regular paint, it's not a problem. Just buy some stain blocker and paint it over the area, leave to dry, then paint your colour over the top.

TO PAINT WOODWORK

If you are painting over an eggshell finish, you can repaint directly onto it – just clean away any dust or dirt before you start. If you are painting over a gloss finish you need to prepare the surface first, to make sure the new paint grips properly – otherwise it will blister and peel away from the shiny layer beneath. There are two options: you can sand the woodwork; or (the less messy and easiest option) paint over it first with emulsion. This adheres well onto gloss and is an excellent primer. Paint over the skirting and doors with the emulsion as you do the walls, and the woodwork will be primed with barely any extra effort.

DECANT AND LABEL YOUR LEFTOVER PAINT

It is really important to reseal the lid on a tin tightly, otherwise rust will develop around the top of the pot. This is a pain because bits of it get in the paint and spoil it. There are two options: brush excess paint out of the lip of the tin before you put the lid back on, and use a wet wipe to make sure there is as little residue as possible; or (and this is my preferred option) decant leftover paint into glass jars and label with the make and name/number of the paint, plus which room you've used it for. The paint looks groovy enough like this to sit smartly on the shelf of the room in question, or you can store it in a cupboard or drawer so that if you need to do a quick touch up, the paint is at hand. It must be airtight so the paint doesn't dry out.

How to fit a dimmer switch

I include this because I don't think many men hanker after dimmer switches, but women certainly do! I spent ages wanting them and thinking I couldn't justify the cost of getting an electrician in to do it. Finally I sorted it out myself, and it took minutes – it really is one of the most basic electrical jobs you can do. If you can wire a plug, you can do this. Before starting any electrical job, isolate the relevant fuses in the fuse box and flick the switch, so there is no power to the socket you are working on. Make sure the lights have gone off! Remove the front plate of the light switch by unscrewing the two screws holding it in place. Gently pull it away from the wall. Hopefully you will see two or three wires going into the light switch, and a back box (the bit the wires sit in) deep enough to take the dimmer switch. In that case, just undo and reattach each wire to the same point on the new switch (the points will be labelled). Check they match up. Dead easy. Job done.

If you open it up and it's not so straightforward, take a photo and take it to your local hardware store, or text it to an friendly electrician for advice. My rule is, if you're not sure, don't guess, ask someone. Advice is freeeee.

DRILLING INTO A WALL YOU WILL NEED:

- **Drill and drill bits**
- **Wire/pipe detector**
- **Wallplugs**
- **Screws**
- **Screwdriver**

First, check you have the right-sized kit for the job. Start with the screw you want to use. Make sure you have the right-sized wallplug for the screw and the right-sized drill bit for the wallplug, otherwise you might drill a hole that's too big or small. Matching drill bit size to wallplug is easy, as the plastic strip the plugs come on has holes that show the drill bit sizes, with the corresponding sizes printed on it. It is also important to check you have the right wallplug type. A regular plastic one will be fine if you are drilling into a solid wall, but that won't grip in plasterboard or a hollow wall – you need special wallplugs designed for these.

Before you start drilling into walls it's a good idea to arm yourself with a cable/pipe detector, which is a little electronic gadget you swipe over the area you're planning to drill into to check it's safe to drill there. It's really easy to use and means you can go ahead and drill worry free. That said, there is a logic to where wires and pipes are behind a wall – they should go directly up or down from where you see a supply point, and then run along the top or bottom of the wall, or under the floorboards. So if you're drilling into a big blank wall away from an electrical or plumbing point, you should be fine. You need a masonry bit for drilling into a wall. Mark the point where you want to make your hole with a cross.

Before you switch on your drill, press the tip firmly into the spot where the hole will be to make an indentation. This will stop the drill slipping when you turn it on, making sure that the hole stays in the right spot. Turn the drill on and make your hole, drilling to the depth of the wallplug. Press the wallplug into the hole. It should fit snugly if you have chosen the right-size drill bit. Fix your screw into the wallplug. As you screw it in, the wallplug opens out, so the screw gets a good firm grip in the wall.

How to put up a picture

First, decide exactly where you want your picture to go. It's good to have someone else around because they can hold the picture in place while you check to see where it looks right. Unfortunately, I am usually far too impatient to wait for someone else, so I use a bit of guesswork. The worst that can happen is that you're slightly off and need to reposition the hook. This can make a bit of a mess, but it'll be hidden by the picture. Anyway, it's very easy to fill and repaint when your guesswork is finally exposed. If you want the picture to be centred exactly on a wall, just measure the width and divide by two to get the centre line, then mark your drill point at the height you want. It's up to you whether you want to be gung ho or more precise.

The easiest way to make sure a picture hangs straight is to hang it from a string or wire across the

★ Wonder Tip ★

If you are hanging several large pictures in a room or along one wall, make sure the distance from the ceiling to the top of the picture – or the floor to the bottom of the picture – is the same for each. It will make the room feel balanced.

back of the frame onto a single hook – that way you can make easy adjustments. It also means the hook is hidden behind the picture. If this makes the picture hang away from the wall, you can make it sit flush by fixing it with sticky tack.

A simple picture hook and pin should be fine in most internal walls – you can get different sizes depending on the weight of the picture. If you can't hammer the long pin into an external wall, use hardwall picture hangers, which you hammer in. If both options fail, drill a hole and use a wallplug and screw.

How to put up a shelf

The most important bit of kit is a spirit level. You really don't want to get to the end of the job and realise the shelf is not straight. The easiest way to put up a shelf is to hold it where you want it, with the spirit level balanced on top so that you can see when it is completely flat. Then draw a faint pencil line under the bottom of the shelf. Now you can hold your shelf support below the line and mark through the screw holes, to show exactly where you need to drill (just poke a pencil through). Check with the cable detector that there's nothing behind the surface that you mustn't drill through, and go for it.

DRILLING A HOLE THROUGH WOOD

It is incredibly useful to know how to drill a large hole through wood. It means you can drill through a wooden surface that something electrical is sitting on and feed cables through it, hiding them so they don't look messy. I love it. It's really simple – you just need your drill plus a special attachment (called a paddle) that you can buy from any hardware store. It is shaped like a flared arrow and comes in various sizes.

HOW TO DEAL WITH A WATER LEAK

Hopefully you won't ever have to deal with a leak, but just in case, you absolutely MUST know where your stopcock is. If you don't, why not check right now so you don't have to worry about it again. You really don't ever want to find yourself running around manically trying to locate it while water is gushing everywhere. In the event of a leak, calmly go and turn off the stopcock, having first stuck some sort of receptacle under the leak, of course. Turning off the stopcock blocks mains water entering the house. Once that's off, turn on the taps to drain the pipes. Now call a plumber. It's sod's law that a leak will happen out of hours, when an emergency plumber will stitch you up with an exorbitant call-out fee, so try to call one you know and trust. If that's not possible, be absolutely clear on their charges before they come. Try to negotiate on the price, by making clear you're not panicked, and so you will take your business elsewhere if their price is too high. There's a whole list of people in the directory, so ring around until you are happy (well, as happy as you can be spending money on something so boring) with the price. While you wait for assistance, don't forget to empty the bucket when it's full.

HOW TO BLEED A RADIATOR

Another of those jobs that sounds daunting but is actually so easy to do. It's worth doing because it makes such a difference to getting your house toasty to the max. You can tell a radiator needs to be bled if it is not hot all the way to the top. All you need is a little radiator key. There are different types, depending on the shape of the little valve on the top right or left of the radiator, so check which you need. If your radiators have been installed in an ad hoc way, as ours have, they probably won't all be the same. So get your radiator key (or keys) and an old rag. Hold the rag around the valve, to catch any water that might spill out. Insert the key and turn it very slowly clockwise. You will start to hear a hissing sound as the air releases. You need to let it out slowly because the water beneath it will be very hot and probably pretty black, so you don't want it spurting out all over the place. Once water starts to emerge, immediately shut the valve tight. Do this to all the radiators to get all the air out of the system. As well as making sure the radiators heat to their full potential, bleeding them should stop annoying bangs and noises caused by air in the system. Bleed once a year when you start to use the heating regularly. It should save you money too, because when the radiators are working to full power you probably won't need to have the heating on so long.

HOW TO STOP A SQUEAKY DOOR

Just apply oil to the hinge, rub well so that it penetrates the mechanism and then remove the excess with a wipe. Check that all the hinges are screwed in firmly. If one is loose, it might be putting strain on another and making it creak.

Cars and
COLD WEATHER

KEEP A STASH OF SPARE ESSENTIALS IN YOUR CAR

I started doing this after we'd driven to the beach for a weekend away and I forgot to take spare contact lenses. I'd also forgotten my daughter's anti-nausea acupressure bands for her carsickness, and we couldn't find any to buy en route. Needless to say, both are now in an emergency stash in the glove box, along with baby paracetamol, antihistamine, plasters, a couple of nappies and baby wipes. You don't need to go over the top. Most things can easily be picked up at a service station, but it's a good idea to protect yourself against forgetting to take something that can't easily be replaced.

JUMP LEADS

I know this sounds fairly tragic, but buying my own set of jump leads is one of the most satisfying and comforting purchases I have ever made! If you've ever been stuck with a flat battery you will know what I mean. You're stranded and helpless, at the mercy of however long it takes for help to arrive. I can't believe it took me two frustrating and time-wasting experiences to finally clock that it is SO EASY to clip on a couple of jump leads and get your car going in literally seconds AND you can buy them very cheaply from any car accessories shop (or online). You will obviously need another car with a working battery (the same voltage as your own) to clip your leads onto and take a charge from – but as long as you've got the leads and know what to do with them, finding a car with a willing and helpful owner shouldn't be a problem. So here's how you do it:

Make sure the car you are using to charge yours is parked adjacent, with the batteries as close as possible (but the cars must not physically touch each other). Just look under the bonnet – if your battery is on the left and theirs is on the right, get the other driver to park accordingly. Basically the leads need to span the gap. Turn off both engines and make sure the cars are out of gear with handbrakes on. Now all you need to remember is RED = POSITIVE and BLACK = NEGATIVE. Clip the red cable onto the positive (+) point on the flat battery. Be careful not to let the clips touch each other at any stage. Clip the other end of the red cable to the positive point on the live battery. Now clip one end of the black cable to the negative (–) point on the good battery, and the other end to a metal earthing point on the engine of the car being charged – a bolt or nut is good (it must be away from the battery or fuel system). Wait 3 minutes, the get the other driver to turn on their engine. Wait a minute or so before you turn on yours. Leave both engines running for about 10 minutes. Turn off both engines and disconnect the leads in reverse order to the way they were connected. Now you just need to drive around for twenty minutes or so to fully charge the battery. How simple but empowering is that?

P.S. If you're in any doubt, it's probably best to hold out for the emergency services. I hope you've got a good book with you!

Stock up on de-icer and a scraper before the cold weather kicks in

We've probably all experienced those mornings from hell when you screech out of the house late for the school run, only to discover the car is completely covered in ice and all you have to scrape it off is a credit card. It takes ages and turns your hands into frozen blocks. Avoid this by buying de-icer and a scraper before the weather gets really cold and stick them in your glovebox. It will pay dividends in smugness when you can breeze out of the house on frosty and snowy mornings and clear your car in seconds. P.S. An empty CD case works brilliantly as a makeshift scraper.

How to drive in snow and ice

Before you move off in snow or ice make sure you have total vision. First, turn on the engine and crank up the front fan and rear window heaters to stop the windows misting up. Then scrape off any snow and spray antifreeze on any frozen windows.

Once you're moving, the key is to drive defensively, to avoid having to stop suddenly. Keep a much longer distance than normal from other drivers. You want to be well clear if they lose control. Drive as slowly as you feel is necessary. Braking hard or accelerating too fast is what makes you skid. When you need to slow down or stop, tap the brakes gently on and off, so that you slow down gradually and safely. It takes ten times longer to stop on ice. If you feel the tyres starting to skid, don't panic. The natural reaction is to slam on the brakes and jolt the steering wheel in the opposite direction. Don't do either! Stay calm, grip the wheel, take your feet off all the pedals so you slow naturally. Once you've stopped skidding, softly tap on the brakes until you stop.

Keep squares of carpet in your boot

Pick up some old samples from a carpet store. These are brilliant to help the car get traction if you're stuck and the wheels are spinning. Just buttress the carpet right up against the front tyres if your car is front-wheel drive, or the back tyres if it's rear-wheel drive. This should get you moving again. (Note: This will work on mud too). In extremis, your floor mats will do the same trick.

How to walk on ice

Put socks or tights over your shoes and it stops them slipping. I know it doesn't look fab, but would you rather look like a fool or feel like one when you fall over? Buy some cheap knee-high stockings and stash them away with the hats and gloves, and prepare to be amazed when you venture out on a snowy day.

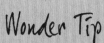

> ### Wonder Tip
>
> *How to use your smart-phone with gloves on! It's so annoying when it's freezing cold, you're wearing gloves and your mobile phone rings, and you can't answer it without taking your gloves off because the touch screen won't work with them on. Well, here's a neat little trick that will change that! Just make the tip of the gloved finger that you use on your phone a little damp and magically it will work. I don't know why, it just does. Don't be precious – the handiest way to do this is to give the glove a little suck – and hey presto, you're good to go! Strangely it only works with wool gloves – not leather.*

Pet's
CORNER

A whiff-free litter tray

Cats must be the easiest pets to look after, because they are – generally – fastidiously clean. The one downside is the litter tray. So here are a few tips to keep it as un-smelly as possible:

- Always scoop out poos as soon as you see (or smell, eek!) them and flush them down the toilet.
- Clean out the tray every five days, before it gets stinky.
- Use bleach to sanitise it.
- Put bicarbonate of soda in the bottom of the litter tray to absorb smells.
- You can quickly freshen up the tray, if you've no time to change the litter (or you're almost out of it), by sprinkling a little bicarbonate of soda over the litter then covering with some fresh litter.

Have an easy-clean pet zone

Whether you go for the ultra residence, or just set aside an area for your pet, put some oilcloth underneath the litter tray and the food and water bowls. It looks smart, demarcates their territory, and makes cleaning up any mess a lot easier because it simply wipes clean.

Wonder Tip

Get rid of pet hair with a rubber glove. Put it on, rub over and hairs will stick to the glove like magic!

Keep a pet planner

Well, not a whole diary for the pet – that would be crazy; this is about simplifying your life – but do make a note of when vaccinations, worming, etc are due, so that you don't forget. Write reminders in the diary at three-month intervals, or however regularly treatment needs to be done, so you don't have to waste any brainpower trying to remember these things.

Stop your pet biting and scratching

When animals are babies, little nips can be quite cute and you don't mind them doing it. The problem is when they get bigger it's not so nice, so don't let them get in the habit. Always keep a toy to hand for a puppy or kitten, and the minute they try to scratch or bite you, give them the toy to do it to. They will quickly learn never to bite or scratch people.

If you're thinking of getting fish...

DON'T! It seems like a fairly good low-maintenance option to quell the children's cravings for a pet. Goldfish are not pets. You can't cuddle them. After about two minutes, no one even bothers to look at them anymore. They just become another chore on your to-do list. I know this sounds brutal, but ask anyone who has succumbed to the goldfish option. I think the problem is that you resent the effort you have to put into feeding them and keeping the tank clean, because there's no love back from them. Whereas a real pet (like a cat or a dog) is more effort, but the reward is exponential.

You love your pets, but you don't love their stuff (or smells) all over the place. How about a little tent for their litter tray, food, water, bed and toys.

HOLIDAYS AND PAMPERING OURSELVES. That probably covers how we'd like to spend all our time in an ideal world. In the real world we know holidays can take a lot of effort to arrange, and pampering can be prohibitively expensive. So we need to think smart to make sure holidays – when we get them – really are relaxing, and to realise that looking after ourselves and being well-groomed doesn't have to cost a fortune.

Getting

Pre-kids you might have been the sort of person who never even thought about where you would lay your head on holiday until you were there. You probably never booked anything until a matter of weeks before heading off. No need to. You could go any time, with no tedious concerns about sticking to school holidays and the extortionate peak-time premiums that come with that. Post-kids, there's just one big fat rule. If you want to have a stress-free holiday, it's all about...

THE PLANNING

If you know exactly where you want to go, always book it as soon as you possibly can. It doesn't cost you any more to book early, but saves the frustration of not being able to stay where you want if you've left it too late, and the time and effort of looking for an alternative. This applies to everything from camping to cottages. Basically, if something works

for you as a family, chances are you won't be the first to have worked out its appeal, and it's first come first served in the tight bookings window of the school holidays. If you want to go abroad, and don't have a specific place in mind, think laterally to get the best value for money. High season doesn't span the same months everywhere, and low season doesn't always mean bad weather. Going somewhere out of another country's season is a great way of making a holiday affordable. Counter-intuitively, it can mean it's cheaper to head further afield and get a great deal on accommodation, rather than pay top whack for a room closer to home. Obviously you need to take into account flight duration and time zones if you are travelling with little ones.

How to get a good deal

If you're planning to stay in a hotel, I'm hoping you already know that the 'rack rate' is just what they aspire to charge. Unless the hotel is the hottest location on the planet and everyone's falling over themselves to snag a room, and you really refuse to contemplate anywhere else, you should NEVER EVER pay the rack rate. Negotiate and aim to pay about 20% less. Just tell the hotel what your budget is (not to cheeky!), be polite, and you should be able to strike a deal. If you are booking flights and accommodation, you need to know that you can marry up availability and best price on each. Be as flexible as you can on dates. Travelling Monday to Monday, for instance, can be cheaper (but not necessarily) than Saturday to Saturday. The fees and taxes, which can add a massive premium to airline ticket prices, can vary dramatically across different days of a week, so check all the permutations.

Avert a potential passport fiasco

As soon as you have booked a trip, double-check your passports are in order. Without going into all the traumatic details, I once discovered on a Friday afternoon – when we were due to travel on the Sunday morning – that my passport was missing. Utter, utter nightmare. Thanks to living fairly close to the main passport office, I managed to get a new one issued on the same day after almost having a stress-induced nervous breakdown at the prospect of not being able to go on my dream holiday. As you can imagine, I really did need a holiday after that. So always, always, always check your passports are where they should be, and in date, in plenty of time, just in case.... Some places require there to be at least six months still to run on your passport, so don't get caught out by that either. It's also a good idea to photocopy the photo page with all your details and passport number. Keep the copy folded in your passport. When you travel, pack it separately from the original, just in case your passport gets lost or stolen.

VACCINATIONS

If you need travel vaccinations, book appointments to get them done as soon as you book the trip, so there are no last-minute issues.

CAR HIRE

To spread out the cost, put a note in your diary to remind you to book the car hire six to eight weeks before you travel. Do shop around on comparison websites to get the best deal and do take out excess cover. It shouldn't be a huge amount – but the excess can be enormous, and if you do end up having even a minor scrape, it could be a nightmare.

AIRPORT PARKING

Again, shop around for the best deal, and book your parking in advance. Do it when you book the car hire, so you don't forget. If you can stretch the budget a bit, and the airport offers a meet and greet option, I would really recommend going for it. It is a bit more expensive, but if you're travelling with young kids it makes your life so much easier. You just leave your car kerbside at departures and go straight in, while someone else takes it and parks it for you. Call them when you're collecting your luggage and they'll bring it right outside the door at arrivals.

DON'T FORGET THE PETS

If you have pets that will need to be looked after when you're away, sort it as soon as you book the holiday. If you need to check them into a cattery or the vets, places will be limited and will get completely booked up over peak holiday periods, so make sure you sort it early. If you have fish, buy a feeding block so they won't starve while you're away – you can get them to last for up to 14 days. Much easier than handing over the fish to someone else to look after.

TRAVEL GEAR

There are so many permutations of what you might need to take with you, depending on where you're going, climate, etc, so here are just the basics that apply to all or most trips.

• **Travel plugs** Use a permanent marker to write on them where they are good for (Continental Europe, North America, etc), so you can easily pick out the ones you need.

• **Travel scales** Cheap to buy, and absolutely vital to avoid having to pay excess baggage fees.

• **Luggage labels** Make your own laminated labels with address and contact details. Get some self-laminating label pouches and either print or write out your details on paper to fit. Seal, punch a hole and use an elastic band to attach them to bags, so that they can easily be put on and taken off as required. For security reasons, only put a home address label on for the return journey.

• **TSA padlocks** These can be undone with a master key by customs officials if your luggage needs to be inspected, so if your bag has to be checked, it won't get ripped open.

★ **Wonder Tip**

Keep regular travel paraphernalia in a labelled box file to avoid the palaver of having to track down all the little bits, like plugs and padlocks, every time you need them

THE PACKING

- Divide everyone's clothes across the bags, so that if one goes astray, no one's left with nothing to wear.
- Always travel light. You can almost always do laundry, or get it done, while you're away, so you really don't need to take enough stuff to wear something new each day. It also means that you won't have suitcasefuls of one or two week's worth of dirty clothes to plough through when you get home. Really think about what you actually need. Also, you want to leave space to bring back your holiday purchases!
- Pack underwear in pillowcases to keep it together and make unpacking easier. Then use the pillowcases as laundry bags while you're away. Pile any dirty clothes into them when you pack to go home, so that you can instantly dump them in the dirty washing box on your return.
- Put some empty plastic bags in your suitcase. They take up no space but are invaluable if you need to return home with wet swimsuits or dirty shoes.

WHAT TO TAKE

- If you're travelling with kids, it's a good idea to take a stash of medical supplies – just in case. I always take: travel sickness wristbands, antihistamine medicine (in case of an insect bite or allergy), children's liquid paracetamol in sachets, plasters and wipes.
- Samples of creams and other beauty products. Whenever I'm at a beauty counter I always ask for a sample of the latest products, then I stash them away for travelling. It means that when I'm away I get to use premium products I don't normally buy – for free. If you have fave products you normally use, get sample sizes of those. They barely take up any luggage space, weigh nothing and you don't have to pack them up to bring home again. Mwah.

FOR A BEACH HOLIDAY

- **Fake tan** – if you're pale-skinned, always take fake tan and put it on before you venture out in your bikini. It saves any temptation to frazzle yourself trying to get a real tan.
- **Loads of suncream** – buy online before you go, to get it as cheaply as you can. Suncream is frighteningly expensive, and even more so if you run out when you're away and have to pay the premium local shops will charge, knowing they have a captive market. Pack it in a plastic bag in case of leaks in transit.
- **Two or three empty spray dispensers** – put water in one to cool you off at the beach, and to spritz off sand at going home time. Use another for a home-made mosquito repellant (see Citronella, below)
- **Sunglasses** – a pair of the most uber shades you can afford. No matter how scruffy you look, stick on a pair of Tom Fords or the like, and you'll feel fabulous. Also, take a pair of cheapies to wear in the water.
- **Reusable ice packs** – super useful when it's baking hot. Obviously you can use them to keep picnic food cool, but my fave use is for keeping you and everyone else cool at night! Freeze and put in a plastic bag (to protect against any leaks) and then place in a pillowcase. Take it to bed at night as an anti-hot-water bottle. Pretty cool.
- **Citronella oil** – put a little dish of citronella oil in your bedroom when you're anywhere that has mosquitoes, to keep them out of your room overnight. Make a natural mosquito repellant spray by adding 4 drops of citronella oil to 200ml of water.
- **Lightweight woven cotton towels** – they pack ultra small, are super absorbent, dry quickly and double up as sarongs. Genius.

CAR SEATS

Hiring car seats can be extraordinarily expensive – more than the cost of actually buying them. It's crazy. Therefore it makes sense to take your own. The obvious downside is that they are bulky. There are a few options, which need to be weighed against your luggage allowance or costs. Get the kids to carry their seats as hand luggage. Or put them in a suitcase. Or buy inflatable seats, which can be fairly expensive for the initial outlay, but they pack small, so when you factor in maybe one annual holiday and the number of years the kids will need car seats, they're probably worth it.

Note: I wouldn't suggest taking any other large kiddie accoutrements, but do check that they will be available in the place you are staying when you book (e.g., cot and highchair) and double-check that the place has remembered to sort it a couple of days before you travel.

THE LUGGAGE

Luggage is a total minefield these days, with different airlines applying different rules. Some basic advice to give here is:

● Always make the most of the free hand luggage allowance. If you're really smart about packing you might get away without having to check in bags. The generic maximum hand luggage size is 55 x 40 x 20cm – although do double-check with your airline because some are even meaner with their allowance. Don't forget, anyone who pays for a ticket is allowed a piece of hand luggage, so if you're a family of four or five and travel super light, you might get away with just taking hand luggage. Do weigh up the hassle factor though – juggling little ones and a trail of bags can be a nightmare. It might be worth checking in one or two bags of maximum weight in combination with light hand baggage.

● Check the maximum bag weight allowed and weigh your bags with travel scales. Dead easy and no more sweating at check in, waiting to see if you'll be fined. Don't forget to pack the scales for the home journey.

Wonder Tip

Tie a colourful ribbon onto your bag handles so that you can instantly recognise your bag on the luggage carousel, and make it less likely that someone else might mistake yours for theirs.

Looking

HOW TO WASH YOUR HAIR

I know this seems pretty obvious, but there are a couple of brilliant salon tips that make a big difference. You know how your hair's often much better the day after it's been washed, when some natural oil's returned, than it is on the day, when it can be a bit fluffy and less textured. The trick is to only massage shampoo into the roots of the hair, avoiding the rest. Obviously all of the hair gets wet and the diluted shampoo that runs through the length of the hair will be enough to clean it without stripping it. Do two gentle washes with small amounts of shampoo rather than one full-on lathered-up-to-the-max hit. Conversely, when you apply the conditioner, only put it on the ends of the hair. The roots don't need it and too much will just make the hair flat.

A tip for washing hair that's really long. To avoid tangles and make brushing easier, comb through while the conditioner is on, then rinse out, and blot dry with a towel (don't rub or it will tangle up again).

★ Wonder Tip ★

The easiest way to avoid using too much shampoo is to use a foaming pump dispenser. You just put a small amount of shampoo into the bottle and top up with water, and it converts the shampoo to foam as it is dispensed. It will save you a fortune on shampoo too, because one bottle will last ages this way.

HOW TO BLOW-DRY YOUR HAIR

Giving yourself a decent blow-dry can be tricky, especially if you've got long hair. Forget about trying to do it the salon way with a big round brush and hairdryer; it's almost impossible to do on your own hair – far too much contortion and aching wrists involved. A hot air styling brush is the secret weapon, whether you've got long or short hair. As long as you buy one that gets very hot, you can quickly and easily blow-dry your hair with volume and body. You can also easily revive it with very little effort between washes, so it looks like you've just stepped out of a salon. When you've washed your hair, if you're not in a rush,

92

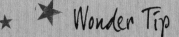

let it dry naturally until it's just very slightly damp. Otherwise, use a hairdryer to get it to that stage. Now you can inject the volume and bounce hairdressers deliver. Wrap hair around the styling brush, turn the heat up to the max, leave it on for a few seconds, then turn it off, or switch to cold air, and hold in place for another few seconds. This means the hair cools while it's lifted away from the roots, which is what fixes the lift. Unroll gently. The hair must be completely dry or it won't fix and the body will quickly drop, so if it's not quite dry, give it another go. This method won't give you curls if you've got straight hair, but if it gives you more of a curl than you want, roll your hair round the brush again, turn it on to top heat and gently pull it away from your head, lifting up and away from the scalp. When the brush reaches the ends of the hair, hold it there and turn off so the hair cools in place. If you want a curl-under on the end, make sure the tips are curved around the brush. If you want dead straight ends, they need to be lying flat on the side of the brush.

THE TOP HAIRDRESSER'S SECRET SPRAY – FOR THE BEST BLOW-DRY FINISH

This tip came from my fabulous hairdresser, who told me that when he worked at one of the most famous salons in the 1970s, they'd style their expensive blow-drys by spritzing beer onto damp hair first. This old-fashioned fix has generally been overtaken by expensive products, but it still works and really is fabulous. You need to use ale – not lager – and decant it into a spray bottle. Spray it on when the hair is slightly damp, not wet. It makes the hair super shiny and holds the style. Don't worry about smelling like a brewery – the alcohol quickly evaporates under the heat of the dryer. Sleek salon-style, oh yeah. (Keep it in the fridge.)

Wonder Tip

Don't be tempted to buy expensive products just because the packaging looks nice on the side. Just repackage the cheapies that you know work, so that they look snazzy. Use pretty little boxes or baskets with lids for storage, or decant into a nice bottle and label up with generic terms like cleanser, moisturiser, etc. I went through a phase of spending a fortune on really expensive shampoo, just because I liked the packaging. It didn't actually work any better. How crazy is that? Just buy a cheap one and rebottle. Don't forget to make use of brilliant pump dispensers, which look stylish and stop you pouring more out of a bottle than you need.

MAKE A GREAT FACIAL OIL

I have probably spent a small fortune over the years on alleged 'miracle' creams. I would say, none have worked – I look no younger than I should, dammit. There was one cream I would have loved to use forever, but it was sooooo expensive it would have been crazy. So I decided to pick the brains of several experts who really know what makes a difference.

The result was a facial oil that I mix up, and which I have found really works in terms of moisturising but not being greasy. I was directed to 'squalene oil', which is produced from olives, although it has no smell or colour and is very light. It absorbs really easily into the skin and is fine to use on all skin types. Our bodies actually produce a version of it naturally, but this starts to decline in our twenties, so it would seem to make sense to put some back in.

The second ingredient is evening primrose oil, which is rich in essential fatty acids and is well known for helping to balance women's hormones. Rose essential oil is an excellent moisturiser. And lavender is antiseptic, anti-inflammatory and soothing, to help prevent breakouts. The oils are not cheap, but what you get by buying them separately and combining yourself is miles better and miles cheaper than anything you can buy ready mixed with them in.

You'll need a scrupulously clean bottle to store your oil in – an old brown medicine bottle, which will protect the oil by keeping out light, is perfect. Combine 50ml squalene oil, 50ml evening primrose oil and 25 drops each of rose and lavender essential oils.

MAKE YOUR OWN BODY OIL

Another area we can spend a lot of money on when we just don't need to. Almond oil and argan oil are both fantastic moisturisers for skin. Just mix up 100ml of each with 20 drops of rose oil for a fabulous-smelling and super-softening oil. Store in a pretty bottle, or a spray bottle for easy application. To give your skin extra sheen, mix with a little liquid highlighter in the palm of your hand before applying. Fabulous.

A CHEAP ALTERNATIVE

Baby oil is a fabulous moisturiser, but if you don't want to smell like a baby, just spritz in some of your favourite perfume. Super cheap, beautifully scented body oil that works.

SHAVE WITH OIL

Again, use any oil you have to hand – olive, baby, etc. Apply and shave. Simple and it leaves your legs smooth and silky. Mmmm. You can do it in or out of water, so it's practical too. If you suddenly find the weather's got warm and you really want to wear a skirt with no tights but haven't shaved all winter, you can shave in seconds without getting wet.

TURBO-CHARGE THE MOISTURISING POWER OF FACE AND BODY OILS AND CREAMS

Oils and creams absorb much better into the skin if it isn't completely dry, which makes sense when you think about it. To moisten your face, either lightly spritz with water (just put mineral water in a spray bottle and keep in the bathroom), or wipe over your skin with aloe vera juice on some cotton wool before applying moisturiser.

It is so easy to mix up your own
really fabulous face and body oils.

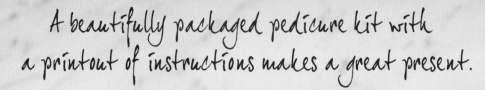
A beautifully packaged pedicure kit with a printout of instructions makes a great present.

GIVE YOUR TOENAILS A PERFECT PAINT JOB IN FIVE MINUTES FLAT

A proper salon pedicure is one of those luxurious treats that should be obligatory on your birthday every year! There's something so fabulous about having your feet massaged and primped by someone else. Unfortunately a pedicure is expensive and time-consuming, so for most of us it's not something to be done regularly. Luckily it is very easy to make your feet look like they've had the Rolls Royce treatment with a little bit of effort at home.

For the fundamentals, scrubbing once a month with a foot file is a good discipline to get into. It doesn't take very long and that way your feet should stay pretty soft all the time. For the best foot scrub ever, get a handful of bicarbonate of soda, add a little water to make a paste and rub all over your feet and lower legs. It's not the most glamorous of scrubs, but the result is amazing! Taking care of the nails is obvious – a basic file is all you need. And orange sticks are perfect for pushing the cuticle down.

But the most satisfying part is how quick and easy it is to give yourself a salon-style paint job, armed with a few great tips. First, make sure the nail is completely clean (any oil or cream will stop the polish getting a good fix), by going over with cotton wool and nail varnish remover. Next put on a base coat. This is really important because it stops the colour absorbing into the nail and makes removing it for next time so much easier. Go straight on with the colour. Make sure the brush is well coated, and keep loading as you need. You want it to be thick, because that's how you get the perfect sleek and glossy look. Be careful not to let the colour leach into the cuticle and skin around the nail – keep the edges clean by scraping a fingernail around if necessary. No need to leave to dry between coats – go straight on to a second coat.

Wonder Tip

Now for the best part – two hero products which are the key to sealing your perfect paint job – a quick dry anti-chip topcoat and quick dry oil. These react with the polish (however thick) – and the double whammy of using both products means the paint should be hard and ultra-shiny in five minutes, touch-dry in about two. There's no need to wait for the polish to set before applying the topcoat, but wait a minute or so to let it set slightly before applying the oil. The nails should last for weeks without chipping. Take these with you if you do go out for a pedicure, to stop your toes getting smudged when you put your shoes on – beauty salons don't always use them.

Scrub up with a muslin

If you've had babies, chances are you've got loads of old muslins lying around. If not, buy some – you can buy a whole stack online very cheaply. Anyway, these beauties are about to become one of the most indispensable elements of your skin care regime. Use them as a washcloth for your face morning and night. The texture of the fabric is perfect for gently exfoliating skin, leaving it looking as fresh and scrubbed up as a child's and feeling baby-smooth. Ooh yeah.

Exfoliate with bicarbonate of soda

This is an amazing exfoliator – and the cheapest! Is there no end to the talents of the humble bicarb? If you are not sure, try it first on your feet, but it is so gentle, you can use it everywhere, including on your face. Keep a large jar in the bathroom and do a body scrub in the shower and a facial scrub once a week. Just put some in your hand and moisten with a little water.

Use nappy cream to zap your zits

You know how miraculous zinc cream is on a baby's red bottom. It's just as great on spots. Try it.

Give dry, dull skin a boost with a cream highlighter

Fake luminous skin by using a cream highlighter all over your face after the moisturiser. You can use it alone or mix with foundation. It instantly brightens your skin by reflecting the light, and also helps to soften lines. Fabulous!

Remove make-up with baby wipes

These are the make-up artist's staple. Gentle enough for all skin types, but brilliant at removing even the thickest make-up. If you have layered up the mascara, don't rub hard around your eyes – we spend enough time trying to mitigate wrinkles, without helping to worsen them ourselves. Remove heavy eye make-up gently by lightly pressing the wipe into the eye socket and holding for about thirty seconds to soak and soften the mascara. A little baby oil helps too, especially if the mascara's waterproof.

Get super-soft hands and feet with petroleum jelly

Slather a thick layer onto hands and feet, wrap in clingfilm and then cover with socks overnight and your skin will be ultra soft in the morning. Don't forget to do your feet first!

How to wash your hands

When you've cleaned the oven or have been gardening or painting, and your hands are absolutely filthy, the best way to clean them is to rub oil over them (olive oil, baby oil – whatever you have to hand), and then scrub all over with a scrubbing brush. The abrasiveness of the brush should remove all traces of paint or dirt, while the oil will protect your skin so it isn't dry and sore afterwards – which is what happens if you use a scrubbing brush and soap.

How to get a clear head

If you wake up feeling muzzy headed, or have a headache or blocked sinuses, a really simple but extremely effective way of perking yourself up is to do a peppermint inhalation. Just add peppermint oil to a bowl of boiling water, lean over and inhale. Start with one drop and add more if you need, because it's really strong! Don't bother about putting a tea towel over your head – it just makes you feel claustrophobic. A few deep sniffs and you'll feel uber perky. Woohoo.

Book in for a health check

If you have any specific health concerns, always get them checked out. Even if you haven't got any, it's a good idea to have a health MOT periodically as you get older, to check blood samples and flag up any potential problems. If you have high cholesterol, not knowing about it won't make it go away. If you haven't got high cholesterol, or anything else to be worried about, and you're told it as a fact, it's liberating – health anxieties won't start to build in your head. It's a bit like when you were a child and you were too scared to peek under the bed because you thought a monster was hiding there. By not looking, you became convinced there most definitely was one, and then became too scared to get out of bed in case it caught you. If you'd only plucked up the courage to look as soon as the fear started creeping into your mind, you'd have known the monster wasn't real and would have saved yourself all the panic. If it turns out something is lurking, you're empowered to deal with it.

Get your diamonds
sparkling in seconds

Just put a teaspoon of bicarbonate of soda in a cup of hot water. Drop in your jewellery. Leave for about thirty seconds and when you take it out it will be as shiny as new! The solution miraculously dissolves the dirt and grease. Use an old toothbrush if you need to give a little extra scrub.

Keep your bag clear

As we all know, handbags are a haven for all sorts of junk you really don't need to carry around all the time. It's so satisfying when you give the bag a good clear out, so that you can easily find what you need. Here are a few bag tips that help keep me organised:
- Use a fairly small bag, just big enough to fit the essentials.
- Have a small purse just for coins and notes, and a separate card holder – one of those plastic flip cases – so that you can easily find the card you're looking for.
- Keep an envelope or small purse in your bag for receipts. Bin receipts you don't need to keep straight away, and put the ones you do need in the envelope.
- Keep your hands free with a cross-body bag. Plus, they don't wreck your posture by weighing you down on one side.

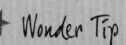

Wonder Tip

If you wear glasses, keep a piece of microfibre cloth (cut a 10cm strip off the end of a large one) in your handbag, to keep them clean. Trying to wipe them with anything else just smears the grease around!

Confidence
AND POISE

STAND TALL FROM YOUR STOMACH

Poise is what sets some people apart from others. When someone walks into a room and naturally commands attention, it's because their air of confidence and ease gives a certain command. Take a look at Kate Middleton – future Queen of England. She is beautiful, but so are a lot of people. She has something else that really sets her apart – and it's poise. I don't know if she was born with it. I guess some people are, but most of us aren't. Luckily it's never too late to learn. We've all been told 'shoulders back'. Actually I think that's counterproductive when it comes to posture and confidence. You're going to

need to get naked to see why.

Take off your clothes and stand next to a full-length mirror – or one where you can at least see from your head to your thighs. First of all, don't alter your natural posture in any way – just observe how you stand. Now thrust your shoulders back – as we're told we should. What happens? Your stomach automatically pots out and actually it all looks and feels rather uncomfortable. Now just contract your stomach muscles. See what happens? By pulling in from your core, everything else suddenly aligns. And, more than that, you look slimmer and taller. Think of your stomach as the posture control centre. You can get dressed now!

Sit at a chair and pull in your tummy. Try and slump at the same time – it's impossible! It might not come naturally at first, but getting back control of your centre really will transform the way you hold yourself and how you feel. Get into the habit – and quite quickly, as the muscles get stronger, you won't need to think about it anymore. When you walk into a room and you're feeling self-conscious, tighten your tummy muscles – suddenly you'll look and feel anchored and in control. If you don't have confidence, fake it, and soon you'll fool yourself too!

HOW TO HAVE YOUR PHOTOGRAPH TAKEN

I spend hours in front of TV cameras every day without thinking about it, but the minute someone tells me to smile in front of a still camera I feel self-conscious, and my shoulders slump as I try to shrink away, not really knowing where to look. Like a lot of

- Angle yourself slightly to the camera. Put your hands loosely on your hips if you're not using them for anything else – it will draw back your shoulders, giving a better silhouette.
- Look directly into the lens. Smile or don't – however you feel comfortable. Mwah!

HOW TO WALK IN HIGH HEELS

Cheat! As someone who is short (1.6m) and could never walk in high heels, it took me a while to work out that I could do it if I bought the right style of shoe or boot – basically something with a lift at the front, to reduce the real heel height. I'm not talking crazy platforms, but a style that gets produced year in year out, regardless of fashion; you just need to seek them out. No more aching feet or hobbling along uncomfortably. Work out the net height (heel minus any lift at the front) you are comfortable walking in. For me it's 6cm, so anything under that is fine without the front lift. Just try various options in the shoe shop. Always remember, if it's not comfortable there, it never will be. The other thing to remember is: let your heel hit the ground first. Walk in front of a mirror and you'll see what I mean.

AND HOW TO GET LONGER LEGS

Again, cheat! Just wear nude shoes to match the colour of your legs – or match shoes to the colour of your tights or trousers – and it automatically streamlines and elongates the legs. Incidentally, nude shoes go with everything, so they are a supremely useful asset to your wardrobe.

people, I have always hated having my photograph taken. Then one day I saw a fantastic photograph of the designer Tory Burch in a magazine and it was a eureka moment. She was standing in a room. Nothing special about where she was or what she was wearing, but the image was so striking. Standing slightly angled to the camera, looking coolly down the barrel of the lens, she was channelling the "Red Carpet-pose" vibe, but in a mundane setting, and suddenly I realised the "Power of the Pose" could be used in any context. I saw in an instant that it's not what you look like (although she is beautiful), but how you present yourself. So here are the tips I gleaned from that photograph:

- Stand tall from your stomach – it immediately infuses you with confidence and makes you look five kilos lighter than if you slump.

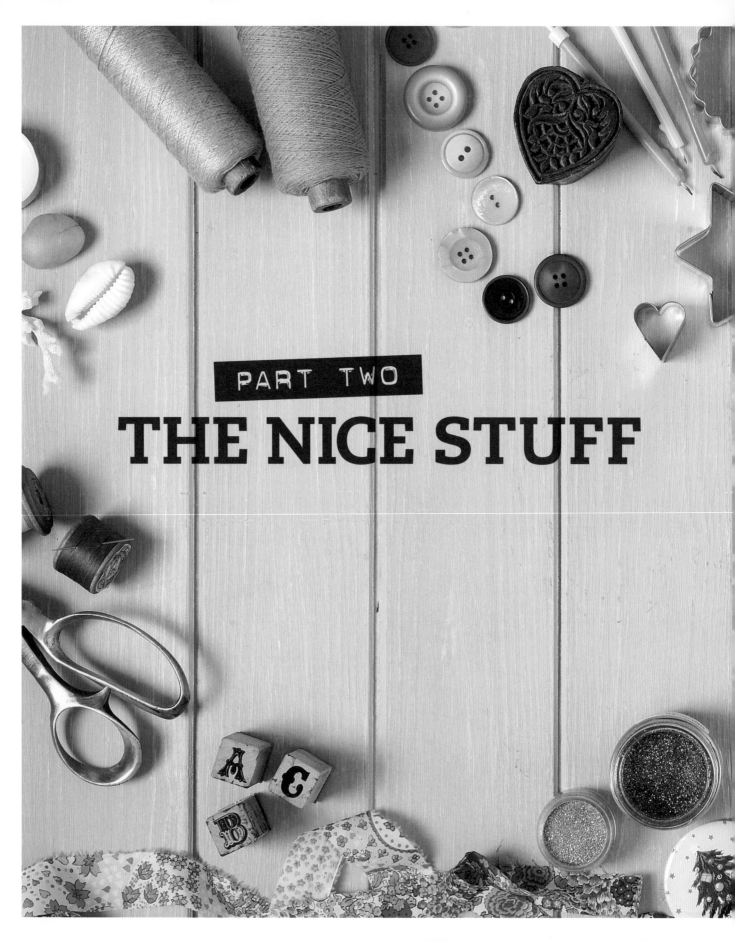

PART TWO

THE NICE STUFF

THIS PART IS ABOUT THE STUFF THAT MAKES YOUR HEART SING,

the nice stuff. Here the 'minimum effort, maximum return' mantra gives way to an equation that is 'the return is worth the investment'. In other words, it's the opposite of corner-cutting and job avoidance. It's about doing stuff that doesn't have to be done but is worth doing for so many reasons. You can so easily create things that will make your home a nicer place – the sort of stuff that can be expensive to buy. But more than that, it genuinely is nicer to make your own. I promise an hour or two spent making something is so much more satisfying than going to the shops and spending money on something similar. The process of making is soothing and therapeutic as your head clears and you forget other pressures. It changes material things from being about acquisitive materialism and money spent, to a reflection of time well spent. Everything in this section is easy to do. I promise you, no special skills are required – just a little time. It's not about making things perfectly – worrying about that is what makes us think we can't do stuff and stops us even getting started.

Make
AND DO

IN A BOOK that is about helping women to cope when they already have too much to do and too little time, you might wonder why I'm such a big fan of making things – of creating extra work. In a counter-intuitive way, this is also about simplifying your life. It's about slowing down. We want so much we don't actually need. Making things yourself helps you to distinguish what's important.

Things
TO GATHER

You don't have to rush out and buy all of these things at once. I have slowly gathered my supplies and equipment over time. Some are not cheap, but in the long run you will save so much money (and get so much pleasure) by making things yourself.

- **Stampers and coloured inks** I absolutely love stampers! I use them to make labels and cards and just love the hand-printed style. Start with an alphabet set and slowly build a collection. Indian carved wooden blocks are fantastic too for printing paper or fabric. All of these can be picked up online (sometimes very cheaply if you're lucky).

- **Sewing machine** You can pick up a really basic sewing machine very inexpensively – that's all I use. You just need something that does simple stitches. The ethos of this book is that nothing requires specialist knowledge or skill. After all, I have neither, but I am good at working out ways of making things simply. It means you won't get the niceties of things like overlocked edges – we'll leave that to the professionals. Literally all I know about using a machine is how to set up the thread and do basic straight stitches of varying lengths, how to wind bobbins and how to do reverse stitches, and I taught myself by reading the manual. If you've never used a sewing machine before, please don't be daunted – it really is very easy and using one is life changing! You could, of course, make do with sewing by hand, which can be satisfying in itself, but it will take a lot longer. That might take some things into the realm of 'life is too short'.

- **Pinking shears** A secret weapon that allows you to cut fabric and use it without having to hem because the zigzag finish naturally prevents fraying. Genius!

- **Empty jars** Get into the habit of seeing jars as a free gift that came with the contents you bought them for, and don't ever throw one out. With a little creativity, glass jars and bottles can be transformed from unexceptional everyday objects into something special that will give pleasure.

- **Preserving jars** These are a bit posher if you're giving something as a gift.

- **Double-sided tape** Another indispensable item for corner-cutting crafting.

- **Permanent spray glue**

- **Giant roll of brown kraft paper** Another of my favourite bits of kit because it's stylish, gets used all the time and is a total bargain. If you buy a 225m roll (I know!) you will have a supply of wrapping paper for life for a teeny-tiny fraction of what you would spend on shop-bought paper. Buy the 90cm width, so you never need worry again about how on earth you are going to wrap over-sized presents – it's a cinch. One warning: the roll is bulky and heavy, so if you don't have anywhere to stash it (hidden behind or under something), you should probably buy a smaller roll from a craft shop, which will work out more expensive but will be more practical. If you're going for the big beast, buy online and go for the 90gsm quality, which is heavy duty and won't tear.
- **Stash of fabric** Think creatively about sources for your fabric because it can be expensive. Markets and independent fabric shops can have great bargains. If there's a particular fabric you're after, search online – often you will find an off-cut very cheaply, which might be enough for what you want. A general trawl of off-cuts and vintage cloth is a great way to source some fabulous pieces, if you've a little time to while away online. Don't forget old clothes too. Sometimes I've bought something because I love the fabric, but then never really wear it. Stash it. You could make something really beautiful from it. Home-made felt is fabulous too. If you're like me, you have probably experienced that sinking feeling when you realise you've accidentally put a woollen item on a hot wash and it's emerged shrunken and thick. Don't throw it away – keep it to make something from. And remember, even the tiniest scraps can make something (see fabric pegs on page 133).
- **Label embosser** One of those things you probably had when you were a kid to produce sticky plastic labels with hammered-out letters. I loved mine then and I adore it now! You can buy one to use with plastic strips very cheaply online or in stationery shops.
- **Art card** Keep a supply of A4 art card and you will always have the wherewithal to make cards and thank you notes. Up to 175gsm weight card will go through the printer if you want to make photo cards.
- **Envelopes and stamps** A full stationery cupboard or drawer is a satisfying thing. It means that when inspiration or urgency strikes and you want to get something in the post, you've already got a stack of envelopes and stamps to hand and can mail without delay or hassle. Talking of stamps, always keep a large supply, plus some scales and a tape measure, so you can avoid the faff of going to the post office by checking mail prices online.
- **Photo printer** You can buy printers really cheaply, and if you use them for making your own cards and notes, the cost will be repaid very quickly.
- **Cookie cutters galore** All sizes and shapes. Brilliant for making potato stampers (see page 159).

Set aside a drawer for your treasure trove of craft tools and materials.

Fabulous New Uses
FOR OLD JARS

This quick tip first of all on preparing your jars. Use baby oil or lighter fluid to remove any sticky residue left behind on a jar after you've scrubbed off the label.

PAINTED TEA LIGHT HOLDERS

These are so easy to make, but look very interior designy because you can match them exactly to your paintwork – or use any vibrant, funky, or muted colours you like. All you need are some empty jars and some leftover paint. Pour a little paint into each jar and swill it around so that it completely covers the inside of the jar. Pour out any excess. Wipe carefully around the rim of the jar with a baby wipe or damp cloth. The paint should come right up to the top of the inside of the jar but the lip and outsides should be clear. Leave to dry. The shiny glass exterior suddenly looks like beautiful porcelain.

BEAUTIFUL LACE TEA LIGHT HOLDERS

This is such a simple thing to do, but it looks really effective. All you need is some old jars – any size – some double-sided adhesive tape and some lace. Wrap the lace around the jar and cut to size. Stick a piece of double-sided tape to the jar and secure each end of the lace to it. Ribbon or strips of fabric would work well too. Make a whole load and group together for a fantastic table centrepiece or line them up along a shelf or the mantelpiece.

SIMPLE HANGING LANTERNS

Hang these from trees or looped over a wire suspended between two points for simple, romantic style. All you need are some empty jars without lids, thin wire and tea lights galore. Cut a length of wire that is long enough to wrap around the rim of the jar, plus an extra 5cm. Cut a second piece of wire to form the loop – decide how long you want the hanging loop, and add an extra 6cm. Fix one end of the loop wire about a quarter of the way along the rim wire, by twisting about 3cm around the rim wire several times. Do the same with the other end of the loop wire, to form the loop. Place the rim wire around the rim and twist the ends together so that it holds tight. Bend the twisted wire back against the rim. Make several, suspend, and light the little candles inside, so they twinkle and glow as they drift softly in the wind.

FILL THE GARDEN WITH JAM JAR TEA LIGHTS

A stunning and so-simple way to light up the outside at night. All you need are as many empty jars as you can muster, plus tea lights. Try to buy long-life tea lights so that they burn for the duration and dot or cluster them around outside. Definitely a case of more is better.

BLACKBOARD TEA LIGHT HOLDERS

Fabulous and fun. Just paint the outside of a glass jar with several layers of blackboard paint. Perfect for a romantic evening – you could scribble little love notes on the outside. Or use them for unusual place names when you're entertaining – just write everyone's names on jars, put in tea lights and place them where you want your guests to sit.

Wonder Tip

Turn cheap tea lights into fabulously scented candles by putting a couple of drops of essential oil or spraying a little perfume onto the wax before lighting the candle. Don't worry about the alcohol in the perfume – it will burn off in about a second.

MATCH STRIKER JAR

YOU WILL NEED:
- Empty jar with a lid
- Two big boxes of matches, or several small ones
- Double-sided tape
- Spray paint
- 5cm heart template (use a cookie cutter)

Spray-paint the lid of the jar – any colour you fancy. A couple of coats should be enough to give good opaque coverage. Cut out the match striker strips from the side of the packets. Cut four 6cm-long strips. Stick them next to each other on a piece of double-sided tape, so that they form a square measuring 6 x 6cm, with tape covering the underside. Draw a heart shape on the underside and cut around it. When the lid is dry, peel away the covering on the tape, and stick it on the lid. Fill the jar with matches. So pretty and practical. Lovely.

CUTE-AS-A-BUTTON JAR

Somewhere stylish to keep your stash of spare buttons so they don't get lost or forgotten.

YOU WILL NEED:
- **Jar plus lid (metal not plastic)**
- **Sandpaper**
- **Wire wool**
- **Stash of spare buttons**
- **Double-sided tape, or glue**

Rub over the spray-painted surface of the metal lid with sandpaper. When you've removed as much paint as you can with the sandpaper, switch to the wire wool, to remove the last traces of paint and to smooth the surface. Now decorate the lid. You could use several small buttons to trace out a heart shape, or just go for one large button – whatever you fancy. Either way, stick double-sided tape or glue to the underside of the button(s) and then stick it/them onto the lid. Now fill your jar and your stash of spare buttons can sit proudly on a shelf, not hidden away in a drawer, forgotten and never used.

PRETTY SWEETIE JARS

These look so effective and make lovely little gifts, or donations to the school fair.

YOU WILL NEED:
- **Old jam jar**
- **Sweets**
- **Square of fabric**
- **Double-sided tape**
- **Ribbon or string.**

Use pinking shears, if you have them, to cut out a square of fabric, with sides measuring the diameter of the lid, plus 6cm. Cover the top and sides of the lid with double-sided tape or glue and then stick the fabric to it. Fill your jar with sweets, screw on the lid, and tie a ribbon or string around. How cute is that?

STRING/RIBBON DISPENSER

Cut a hole in the lid of your jar using a wood chisel – rest the lid on a wooden block and hammer on the chisel to cut through the metal. Cut a piece of fabric that will cover the top and sides of the lid. Cover the lid with either glue or double-sided tape and fix the fabric to it. When it has dried, cut the fabric away from the hole and use scissors to trim around the lid. Put your ribbon or string into your jar, thread the end through the hole in the lid, screw it on and you have a very pretty and practical dispenser.

MONEY JAR

Piggy banks are about saving money, so why spend precious pennies on buying one, when you can easily make a fabulous and stylish one for free?

YOU WILL NEED:

- **Jam jar with a metal lid**
- **Hammer and a wood chisel**

(they're sharp, so will cut through metal)

- **Glass frosting spray**
- **Cut-out paper template**
- **Fabric to cover the lid**
- **Double-sided tape, or glue**
- **Craft knife**

Start by choosing your design for the jam jar. If you are making one for a child, their initial is a good idea, so that they can clearly identify their own stash. Otherwise a simple star or heart works well. Or any shape you like, of course. The easiest way to create a large letter template is to open up a blank page document, type the letter of your choosing and scale it up to the size wanted. Now go through different fonts until you find one you like, print and cut out. Cover the back of your paper cut-out with double-sided tape, and stick it onto the jar. Spray the jam jar with frosting spray. Leave to dry, according to the instructions on the can. Make a slot in the lid, measuring about 3 x 0.8cm. Put a block of wood under the lid, place the chisel on the surface and hammer it firmly to cut cleanly through the metal. The cut-out strip should just pull away. If not, cut through it with scissors. Make sure there are no jagged edges by bending any flaps back on the underside. Cover the top and sides of the lid with double-sided tape, or glue. Cut a piece of fabric large enough to cover the top and sides of the lid and stick it on – trimming the edges to neaten. Use a craft knife to cut away the fabric from the coin slot. Once the frosting spray has dried, peel off the template and tape, to reveal a stylish clear window through which you can see your stash of coins grow. Screw on the lid, and start filling up.

WASP TRAP

An old-fashioned method that helps keep wasps at bay. If you're bothered by wasps when you're sitting out, just get an old jam jar and pour in a 50–50 mix of sugar and water. Add a tablespoon of honey to make it nice and sticky, for good measure. Cut a square opening (about 3cm squared) in the lid of the jam jar, using a small wood chisel. Place a wooden block under the lid and hammer on the chisel to cut through the metal. Place the jar away from the table so you can relax while the wasps are diverted from your spread, unable to resist the sweet temptation.

TEA CADDIES

There's something very soothing about getting cupboards and drawers in order. Use big old jars to store tea bags, coffee, chocolate powder, etc. Just remove the sticky label, add a home-made plastic label and fill. Now you'll be able to see at a glance exactly what you've got, and what you're running low on. And it looks stylish to boot. We all know a cup of tea can work wonders, especially when you're channelling the whole coffee shop at home vibe….

A Spot

OF SEWING

BASIC HAND STITCHES

SLIP STITCH

Possibly the most useful stitch you could learn because it means you can sew up seams invisibly. First, knot your thread and pull it up through from the underside of the seam. Pinch the seams together between your forefinger and thumb. Now imagine a continuous 's', zigzagging between the two sides, joining them together unseen. Weave your needle in and out, entering one seam at the same level you have left the other, then exiting again two or three millimetres along. Continue until both sides are firmly joined. It is quick, easy and super satisfying when you can admire your very professional hand finish.

BLIND HEMMING

Dead easy. Just create your hem by folding the fabric over twice, so that the fraying edge is inside the hem, and then iron, to hold it. To sew it invisibly, you need to make sure that the needle and thread just snag a little of the fabric each time you go through – enough to hold the stitch, but not so much that you actually see the thread come through. Obviously the underside of the hem doesn't matter, but check each time you make a stitch through the outer edge that you can't see it. Either sew with a longish slip stitch (1cm between staggered needle points) or a wide overstitch.

BLANKET STITCH

A very pleasing stitch, because it gives a homespun finish. Use it on fabrics like felt, where the edges can be left raw without fraying. Pass the needle through both pieces of fabric, from back to front. Loop the thread back over and again pass the needle through from back to front, about 3mm along from the previous hole. Before you pull the thread tight to make the stitch, slip the needle underneath the loop of the thread to catch it. It will pull straight along the edge of the fabric, creating a three-sided box effect as you go. It's a great first stitch to teach children too.

★ Wonder Tip

A genius way to make turning up a hem easy is to staple rather than pin. It's quicker and less fiddly than using pins, especially if you're turning up your own clothes, and trying to pin while wearing the item. Plus, it means that you don't get pricked by the pins when you take off the item, and they will stay put. Remove the staples carefully afterwards by prising them open with a blunt knife. Rub over the little holes in the fabric to move the fibres so the hole disappears.

GET YOUR SCISSORS SUPER-SHARP WITH A PIECE OF TINFOIL

Before you start making anything, make sure your scissors are really sharp – it makes cutting fabrics so much easier. All you need is a piece of tinfoil. Fold it over on itself several times so it is six or eight layers thick. Cut through the foil with the scissors around ten times. Your scissors will be sharp again. Wow!

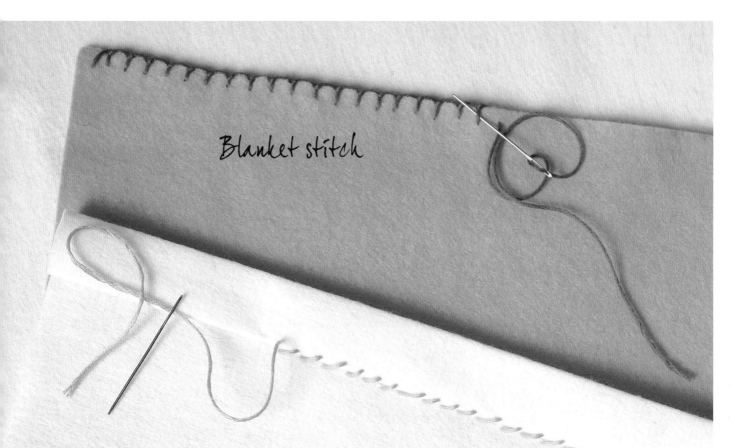

Blanket stitch

Blind hemming

Slip stitch

HOW TO THREAD A NEEDLE
If you're having difficulty threading a needle, pull
a hair out of your head, fold it in half and pass the
loop through the eye of the needle. Pass the thread
through the hair loop, and pull the loop back through
the eye. It will take the thread through with it.

SIMPLE CURTAIN

Basic curtains are so quick and easy to make if you use rings that clip onto the fabric and hang them on a simple pole or a wire. Just cut a length of fabric about 10cm longer than you need. This allows 5cm for hems at top and bottom. You don't need to worry about hemming the sides because of the selvedge. If you are covering a wide area, you could join the fabric together, or else go for the easier option and make several individual lengths to drape together, as I have done here. Hang and admire! These are great – not just at windows – but to cover messy storage areas. Note: striped fabric is great to use because it's easy to tell if you've got straight edges and straight hems – just make sure the lines marry up when you fold the fabric over.

Wonder Tip

To cut a perfect square, or rectangle, out of fabric, use a book to make sure your corners are proper right-angles. Just measure the width or length of your fabric down the selvedge, which you know is straight. Then place a book at the end, and it will show you exactly where the adjacent line needs to go, to be at a perfect 90 degrees. So simple.

THE EASIEST CUSHION COVERS

Making cushion covers is such an easy and satisfying way to update a room. They are so simple and quick to make, and because they use very little fabric you can go for something you really love, but might not be able to afford to use more of. This is the simplest way to make them. No zip required – it's basically a wrap job.

Measure around the cushion pad you are using. Double the length (to cover front and back) and then add on 20cm. So, if you are using a 40 x 40cm square pad, this first measurement will be 40 x 2 + 20 = 100cm. The second measurement is the width plus 5cm (40 + 5 = 45cm). Cut out a piece of fabric measuring 100 by 45cm. Hem the top and bottom of the 100cm length. Fold over 1cm, then 1.5cm at each end and stitch – the double fold prevents fraying. Lay the fabric right way up and fold about 30cm over. Bring up the bottom end and fold, so that the two ends overlap and the cushion is effectively inside out. You need to make sure the cover measures 40cm. Pin down the sides and sew a 2.5cm hem on each side. That's it. Turn inside out and you have your cushion cover.

A SIMPLE LAUNDRY BAG

Laundry bags are a great way to give some order to the dirty washing, so that you are not subsumed by messy piles of clothes. They're one of the easiest things to make, but look really stylish, especially if you do several in different fabrics and hang them next to each other on simple pegs near the washing machine. You will need 1m of 140cm-width fabric. First, cut a 15cm strip off the full length of the fabric, so you have a piece measuring 15cm x 1m. Cut this piece into two – one measuring 10cm wide and one measuring 5cm. Put them to one side. Next, fold the large piece of fabric in half widthways and cut it into two pieces, each measuring approximately 62.5cm x 1m. Sew a hem along the top end of each large piece of fabric (the opening of the bag), folding over 1cm and then again, to give a neat finish. Place the two pieces of material together, with the right side facing in, and machine stitch around the sides and bottom, leaving the top open. Turn the bag the right way out. Fold over each short end of the 10cm x 1m strip of fabric and hem. Then make a hem along the long sides by folding about 1cm over and ironing. Pin this strip around the top end of the bag, about 5cm beneath the opening. Fold it in half and place the centre point on the left-hand seam, so that there is a gap of about 10cm between each end of the strip and the right-hand seam. This is where you will thread the drawstring through. Fold the 5cm x 1m strip of fabric in half. Turn the raw edges under so that they are inside, and then machine down the length of the fabric – this will create the drawstring for the bag. Attach a large safety pin to one end and thread it through the funnel. Sew the ends of the drawstring together and pull the string around so that the sewn ends are hidden, and your bag is good to go. You could make colour-coded sacks for whites, delicates and coloured laundry, or else stamp a label using fabric paint onto the front, if you've used a plain material. Satisfying, practical AND stylish.

DOOR STORAGE BAGS

For most of us, storage space is at a premium, so using the back of doors is a good way to keep things accessible but neat and tidy. These pouches are super simple to make and look so fabulous you'll be happy to have them hanging on the back of every door. Cut out two 40cm square pieces of fabric. Don't forget the selvedge. I always try to save myself a hemming job by using the selvedge for unfinished edges. If you can't make use of the selvedge, fold over half a centimetre or so and then double it over again for neatness to hem along one side of each square. Machine stitch, to make a narrow hem along what will be the opening of the pouch. Now sew the squares together – inside out – around the other three sides. Turn the bag the right way out. Sew loops of ribbon, or fabric, onto the top corners of the bag. Put little hooks on the door and loop the ribbons onto them. If you have used a plain heavy fabric, why not print a label on the front with stampers or a stencil and fabric paints? If you have used a light or patterned fabric, you could make up a label stamped on a separate piece of linen or heavy cotton and stitch it on. Or just leave the bag simple and unadorned. As you like.

LAVENDER BAGS

Home-made lavender bags are so pleasing hanging in your wardrobe or dotted around drawers, and they make simple but thoughtful little gifts. You can run one up in seconds with a sewing machine. Hand-stitching takes longer of course, but can be therapeutic.

YOU WILL NEED:

- Fabric
- Ribbon or a strip of fabric for hanging
- Dried lavender (for the best deal, buy in bulk online)

TO MAKE A HANGING
HEART-SHAPED LAVENDER BAG

Cut out two fabric hearts. A large cookie cutter makes an ideal template. If the fabric is patterned, lay the two pieces together with the pattern facing in. Make a loop with the ribbon or fabric strip that you will use to hang the bag and sandwich it between the pieces of fabric, so that the two ends are poking out of the top where the heart dips – these will be inside the heart. Anchor the ribbon with a couple of hand stitches. You need to sew around the heart, but must leave a little gap of about 2.5cm so that you can pull the material through and turn the heart the right way round, and also to fill it with lavender. It is easiest if the gap is along one of the flat sides, so start sewing about two thirds of the way down the right-hand side. Use a pencil or similar to poke the fabric through the hole and make sure all of the hems have been properly stretched out. Use a teaspoon or a funnel to fill the bag. Finally, stitch the gap closed, using a slip stitch so that it is invisible.

To make a simple square or rectangular lavender bag

Nothing could be simpler. Cut out two pieces of fabric and sew as before. It's great to make these if you want to churn out a load for drawers, or as quick simple gifts. One of my fave fabrics for this is old sari trim. Do a search online and you'll come up with a treasure trove of options.

A cherry stone hottie for cosy toes at bedtime

Cherry stone hotties are a brilliant and safe alternative to hot water bottles – a great option for kids. All you need is some fabric and some cherry stones, which you can buy online. Fake fur, soft fleece or boiled wool from an old jumper are the best fabrics for the outer cover. First make an inner bag to hold the cherry stones, using any old fabric. Cut two rectangles measuring 40 x 30cm. Sew them together with the right sides facing in. Leave an opening of about 6cm. Feed the fabric through the gap to turn it the right way out. Pour in the cherry stones until the pillow is about two thirds full. If you want, you can scent the cherry stones with essential oil. Sew the cover closed. Now make a slip cover in the same way described on page 117 for cushion covers. Microwave the inner bag for 3 minutes, put it inside the slip cover and stick it under the bed cover about 10 minutes before bedtime. Mmmmm, cosy.

Make leggings out of old tights

Actually, this requires no sewing at all, but is a great way to get extra wear out of tights the children have outgrown – a perfect extra layer for spring, which looks funky too. Literally all you need to do is snip off the foot. Cut at the lowest point you can, just above the heel, because they will curl and spring up slightly. It's easier to make them shorter if you want, but if you've cut them too short you can't make them longer again! You don't need to worry about hemming because they will not fray. If you fancy some grown-up leggings, do it with your own tights too. I picked up this tip from a very expensive hosiery store when I wanted a specific coloured pair of footless tights to match a dress. They only had tights in that colour, so they just snipped the feet off in front of me!

Change the buttons on a cardigan or jacket

This is a lovely way to freshen up an old stalwart, plus it gives you a great excuse to indulge in a good browse around a haberdashery – old fashioned, simple and inspiring. If you can't get to one easily, go online and knock yourself out. Entrée des Fournisseurs is one of the finest haberdasheries I have come across. It's in Paris, but luckily they have a brilliant website and will ship anywhere. Otherwise just do a general search on buttons – maybe vintage – to unearth all manner of little beauties. The fun part is tracking down something you love. They do, of course, have to be sewn on, but here is a little tip to make that part easier. To make sure the button isn't sewn too tight against the fabric (which makes it almost impossible to do up), lay a spare needle or toothpick over the top of the button so that the stitches pass over that as you bring the needle up through the underside of the button and back down underneath. When you've done about six to eight loops attaching the button to the fabric, remove the object from the top of the button and pull the button up so that there is a gap between the button and the fabric. Wind the cotton tightly around the threads to hold the button slightly apart from the garment. Pass the needle through to the underside and secure. Sweet.

There is something very therapeutic about curling up and doing a spot of sewing.

HOW TO SALVAGE SOMETHING THAT'S BEEN ATTACKED BY MOTHS (OR ANYTHING IN NEED OF REPAIR)

First of all, use some invisible thread to stitch the hole together, trying not to pull so tight that the wool or fabric puckers. Obviously you could leave the repair job at that if you don't fancy a frippery. Otherwise there are loads of ways to turn a dull repair job into something more creative and pleasing. You could cut out a pretty bit of lace or fabric and sew it on – a simple little patch, or make a feature of it. For instance if the hole is on the cuff, maybe stitch a band of lace, ribbon or fabric around both sleeves. Another sweet alternative is a little ribbon bow. Tie a bow out of a piece of ribbon. Sew through the knot to attach it onto the repair area, then stitch a line down the middle of each piece of the bow, to fix it securely. Depending on whether you want to make a feature of it or not, you could make a small or large bow. Another option is to sew little beads or sequins over the area – either forming a shape, or just randomly.

BUNTING

Bunting is such a simple way to jazz up a room, either for a party, or just for decoration, to bring a flash of colour. Don't buy it because it is so cheap and easy to make.

All you need is fabric – mix and match or just go for one pattern or plain, as you wish – and some 25mm cotton tape, which you can buy very cheaply in a haberdashery or online. Cut the fabric into 20cm-wide strips, across the width of the fabric. (You will have pieces measuring 20 x 140cm, or whatever the width of the fabric is.) The fabric will fray a little with ordinary scissors, but I like the slightly scruffy look. If you're worried about fraying, use pinking shears.

Now cut triangles from the strips by criss-crossing the material with the scissors, so that all of the fabric is used. Don't worry about making the triangles an exact or identical shape or size – variations add to the homespun charm. One strip will give you enough triangles to make about 4.5 to 5 metres of bunting, depending on how wide a gap you leave between the triangles when you stitch them onto the tape.

Machine stitch the triangles onto the tape. No need to pin them into place, just keep the stitch running the full length of the tape, and position triangles as you go. Use quite a large stitch. If it pulls tight against the tape, when you have finished, and before you tie the loose ends, stretch the tape out to loosen the stitches. That is it. If you're doing it for a party, make as many metres as you can bear, because you can never have too much!

TABLECLOTH DEN (See picture overleaf.)

This is such a funky tablecloth – great for children's parties, although ours normally hangs around long after the party's over because the kids (and cat!) love hiding out and playing in it. Choose any fabric you like, but the cheaper the better because, depending on the size of your table, you might need up to six metres. If you've got any remnants, or old sheets, they work brilliantly stitched together to make contrasting panels.

You're basically going to stitch together five rectangles. Measure the top of your table and add 6cm to the length and width to allow for 2cm seams, plus a little give in the size. Cut a piece of fabric to these measurements. This will form the top of the cloth. Then measure from the top of the table to the floor and add 3cm. Cut two rectangles of fabric measuring the same length as the top piece x the top to floor length. These will form the two long sides of the den. Cut two more pieces measuring the width of the top piece x the top to floor length. These will form the short sides of the den. Machine stitch the top of each panel to each side of the tabletop piece. Do not worry about hemming the bottom or sides of each panel. Place the cloth over your table and then decide where you want the den door to be. Cut from the floor to about 10cm below the tabletop. If you use pinking shears it will help to prevent fraying. You can leave the entrance as it is, but a sweet touch is to cut a length of wide colourful ribbon (5cm is perfect), fold and pin around the raw edge and stitch it on.

To finish off, pin bunting around the tabletop. See left for how to make quick and easy bunting. Don't worry about stains. Of course you can wash the den cloth, but anything that won't come out can easily be covered with pretty patches – squares, hearts, stars, flowers – which will make it even cuter!

A lovely way to remember a holiday.

All You Need is

A LITTLE BIT OF FABRIC

A FABRIC PHOTOGRAPH CONCERTINA

This is simple, stylish and practical – the perfect combination! All you need to make one of these is some fabric, some card (from an old cereal box is ideal), permanent spray glue and photographs. For the best result opt for photographs that are all the same size and layout, but you can mix and match if you want. Cut out rectangles of card the same size as each photograph. Cut a piece of fabric to use as the backing – the size will depend on how many photographs you are using and their shape and size. Basically, you want a 1cm gap between photographs and for the fabric to span the top and bottom of each photograph exactly, with no border. So, if you use six photographs, each measuring 15 x 10cm, the fabric needs to measure 95 x 10cm. You do need to use an even number of photographs, so that when the concertina closes, the photographs are all on the inside. Now stick each of the photographs onto the pieces of card, then stick the card to the fabric. Make sure they are level along the bottom, leaving a 1cm gap between each. Trim the fabric neatly along the top and bottom of the fabric. That's it. So simple, takes seconds and it's a lovely way to carry photographs around in your bag. It makes a great gift too. If you mount them onto a piece of plain linen, you can stamp a message onto the front cover. Lovely.

FABULOUS FABRIC LACES

I made some of these for my daughter in desperation one morning as we were about to race out of the door and I discovered she'd removed the laces from her shoes, which were nowhere to be seen. In need of a quick solution I cut two strips of fabric and threaded them through. By chance, a practical necessity was suddenly transformed into something fabulously funky! Dead easy. Make some for yourself too!

★ *Wonder Tip*

If your child is always removing laces – or you're just sick of always having to do them up – another option is to replace the laces with elastic. It's quick and easy to do and actually looks really cool, as well as being ultra practical. Just cut two pieces of 1cm-width elastic, the same length as the shoelaces. It doesn't have to be plain white – you can buy all sorts of different colours from a haberdashery. Thread the elastic through as you would do the laces. You want to keep them slightly loose, so that the shoes can slip on and off easily, but not so loose that they just slip off – test them on the child's feet. When you're happy, cut off the excess elastic, and secure the ends together by overlapping them and sewing two rows of tight running stitch. Wiggle the elastic around so that the joined area slips through an eyelet and is hidden. I totally love it!

Don't worry about making these perfect – it's about getting a great result quickly and easily.

Pretty box files

It is so easy to cover anything with fabric, transforming it from a mundane item to something that makes a difference to the feel of a room. Box files are a perfect case in point. Just buy the cheapest box files you can. Cut out a rectangle of fabric (a fairly thin fabric works best) measuring 70 x 50cm. Don't worry about the raw edges – the glue will fix the fabric so that it doesn't fray.

Sit the box file on top of the fabric (wrong way facing down) and adjust its position until the fabric can cover it completely – like wrapping a present. Use a piece of chalk to mark the material around the four edges of the base of the box. If you want to attach ties to hold the box shut, cut two 15cm lengths of ribbon or strips of fabric and glue them onto the top and side of the box where you want to tie them. Glue them on the outside so that the ends will be covered with the material. Now spray-glue over the base of the box. Stick it onto the fabric (positioning it where you made the marks) and smooth out the material so that there are no wrinkles. Spray all the other sides of the box. Now you need to work quickly. Stick the fabric on each side and the lid, pulling it gently (don't stretch it) so that there are no wrinkles and pressing it on firmly. You want the fabric to stick completely along each side, so that a V-shaped piece of material, which you can cut away later, fans out from each corner.

Leave the fabric to fix to the glue for a few minutes. Then use very sharp scissors to trim the excess fabric away – just slide the scissors along the edges of the box to give a clean line and cut away the corners. If the fabric hasn't stuck down properly anywhere, use a little craft glue to fix it. Use stampers to print a label for the side of the box, stamping the ink onto a piece of linen or other fairly thick fabric. Cut out around your word and stick the label onto the spine of the box with double-sided tape. Don't worry about any fraying threads – they add an edge that stops the files looking too chichi. The files look really stylish lined up along a shelf. Filing suddenly becomes appealing – now that's a revelation!

Give your favourite well-worn cookery book a new lease of life with a wipeable cover

Don't you just hate it when your favourite cookery books start to look really manky, thanks to the constant spattering they're subjected to when you're cooking and using them at the same time? Not a pretty sight on the side in the kitchen. Here's a great way of making them look fabulous, and so much more practical, in about a minute!

All you need is a small piece of oilcloth, scissors and spray glue. First, give the cover of the book a good wipe (with some scouring cream if it's really filthy!) to remove any grease. Wipe with a clean damp cloth and dry thoroughly. Open out the book and lay it flat on the oilcloth. Cut a piece of material with a margin of about 2cm all the way round. Then spray-glue over the front and back covers and spine. Now lay the back of the book flat on the oilcloth and press down firmly, making sure there are no wrinkles. Bring the cloth all the way around the book, pressing into any indentations around the spine as you go.

Leave to dry for a few minutes, then cut the excess cloth all the way around the sides of the book. It means you will have raw edges, but that's fine – they won't fray. Punch out a plastic label with a label maker for the spine. Voila – a wipeable and stylish cover to give your fave books a new lease of life. Now they'll look super stylish on the shelf.

How to cover a book

It is so easy to re-cover a book and is really worth doing as it allows you to personalise and prettify. I bet you used to do it at school all the time, to put your own stamp on boring files and books – I know I did. All you need is a can of permanent spray glue, some paper and some sharp scissors. First, cut the paper around the book, leaving a 4cm margin on all sides. Spray-glue over the covers and spine. Place the back cover onto the paper first. Then bring the paper round to fix onto the spine, making sure that it is in direct contact with every part of the book as you go, including the undulations down each side of the spine. Once the paper is fixed onto the front cover, press the paper firmly onto the glue to get a good fix. Fold the edges of the paper inside the cover – you will need to snip down the spine so that the paper will fold around the cover. Glue the folded edges to the cover. To cover the end of the spine, trim the paper so that you have a flap about 1cm long, which you can glue around the top and bottom of the spine (trim a little more obviously, if 1cm is too long). Give the cover a neat finish by cutting out extra pieces of paper to glue on the inside of the front and back of the book. Print the title on the spine with stampers or a plastic label maker, or print out a label from the computer and glue on.

Block Printing

Block printing by hand has to be one of the simplest ways you can elevate something from basic to stylish, with absolutely zero skill required on your part. That is why I love it. It looks so beautiful and intricate, but someone else has done the hard part for you, in making the hand-carved block. Incidentally, I think these blocks are beautiful in themselves, so don't hide

them away in a drawer; leave them on the side or a bookshelf so you can admire them. I promise, once you start block printing and see the endless possibilities of what you can do with it, you'll be addicted! So here are a couple of ideas to get you started:

A HAND-BLOCKED TABLECLOTH

If you have a plain tablecloth you want to transform, great. Otherwise, cut your chosen piece of fabric to size. As you've probably realised by now, I'm a bit of a fan of frayed edges, so I would just leave mine as is. If you want something neater, it will only take a few minutes to hem the edges with the sewing machine. Now for the fun part. Pour your fabric paint into a paint tray. Use a small sponge paint roller (a rad roll). To ensure a good clear print, you need to make sure there is a soft but firm surface underneath the fabric so that it yields slightly, allowing all parts of the engraving to come into contact with the material. A piece of foam is perfect because you can lay the cloth on the table and see the pattern forming as you go. Just move the foam where you need it. Otherwise you can use the ironing board. Roll paint over the block and start printing. I'd have a little practice on a piece of scrap material first, so that you can judge how much paint and pressure you need to apply. Once your masterpiece is done and the paint has dried, fix the paint according to instructions on the packet. Usually you pay a tea towel on top and then iron over.

A HAND-BLOCKED BEDSPREAD AND PILLOWCASES

Block printing is a fabulous way of transforming cheap plain bedding into something special. Just buy very basic plain cotton duvet covers and pillowcases and get printing. Be as funky as you like. How about printing a vibrant orange onto hot pink? Or keep it simple with navy or taupe onto white?

These pegs take seconds
to make but look amazing.

Little
THINGS

SIMPLE STYLISH HANGERS

The free wire coat hangers you get from dry cleaners are great in that they take up very little space in your wardrobe, but they look pretty ugly. With a tiny bit of effort you can transform them from mundane to marvellous, and in the process make your wardrobe look so much more appealing. When you go shopping part of the temptation is that clothes look so much more alluring when they're hanging in orderly colour co-ordinated ranges. So why not give your wardrobe the same treatment? To glam up a hanger, all you need are some strips of fabric and double-sided tape. If you use fabric that is 140cm wide, two 2cm-wide strips should be enough to wrap around the entire hanger. Start at the hook, and stick a piece of double-sided tape around the end. Stick the fabric to it and start twisting, wrapping it around the hanger as you go. When you come to the end of the strip, secure it with a piece of double-sided tape wrapped around the hanger. Attach the next piece and carry on. Finish by sticking the end down with more tape. That's it. These make a lovely gift too. If you are giving someone an item of clothing as a present, throw in a home-made hanger for them to hang it on. Nice.

KEEP A BOOK OF QUOTES

This is a lovely way of remembering the funny or special things the children say. At the time you think you won't ever forget, but then you promptly manage to do so. Buy a hardback book of plain pages, and then personalise the cover. If you can buy one with a plain cover, it is easy to customise with stamps or printed labels. Otherwise, you can cover a book very easily with kraft paper, to give you a blank canvas. This makes a lovely gift for someone with a new baby.

PRETTY PEGS ON A HANGING LINE

Fabulous in a child's bedroom or the kitchen. A really stylish but simple way of displaying photographs, mementoes and the numerous artworks kids produce. All you need is a piece of string or wire, some wooden pegs, double-sided adhesive tape and something to cover the pegs with – wallpaper, fabric, wrapping paper, even pretty prints from a magazine or leaflet. You don't need much because all you want is a strip the size of the peg to cover one side. Lay your peg on the cover material and draw around it. Cut out and stick to the peg with tape. Fix a line of string or wire, and change your display as often as you like.

BEAN TIN PEN POTS

Never ever throw out an empty bean tin. There is something so pleasing about the simplicity of the design – the shiny metal and ribbed band around the middle – and there are so many ways you can make use of them. Giving items a new purpose is the best way to recycle. So, here's how to make groovy pen pots. An array of bean tins, some decorated, others plain, stuffed with colouring pencils and paint brushes is so stylishly utilitarian – my favourite combination! First, clean the cans. There are various ways to decorate. Wallpaper works brilliantly because it is thick and durable. You need such a small piece that you could use a free sample, costing you nothing. Cut out a rectangle measuring 102 x 233mm. That will fit exactly between the lip at the top and bottom of the can. Wrap double-sided tape around the top and bottom of the tin and fix the paper onto it. You could also stick a strip of fabric around the tin, or spray-paint it.

Keep an empty tin alongside the pencils with a sharpener in it and use it as a little bin for pencil sharpenings.

A MORE GROWN-UP VERSION

A bean tin can even grace a posh desk, if you schuzz it up with string. Simply run two strips of double-sided tape down opposite sides, top to bottom from just under and just above the lipped bands at both ends of the tin. Wind natural string around the tin, pressing it onto the sticky tape as you go, to hold it in place. Wrap it tightly, so there are no gaps. Fill the pot with natural cedarwood pencils and you have a stylish and useful desk accessory.

BEAN TIN CANDLE HOLDERS

Another great use for old bean tins. Not original, but groovy nonetheless. First, clean all the sticky residue off your tin. Then fill it with water and freeze. This means that when you hammer holes into the sides, the tin will keep its shape and won't look all bashed in. Once it's frozen, get a nail and a hammer and stamp out a pattern or a shape, or you could spell out a word across several cans, by printing individual letters on them – like L-O-V-E. If you want to hang the candle holder from a tree, hammer holes on opposite sides just under the rim, to thread string or wire through. Let the ice defrost and dry thoroughly. You can either leave it like this, or spray-paint.

Fabulous – and fabulously cheap – framing

Buying picture frames can be really expensive, and they're not usually top of the priority list when it comes to spending money, so too often great pictures lie hidden away in drawers, or never even make it to hard copy. This is a great way to frame photographs very cheaply, but with maximum style. Buy super-cheap clip frames. Remove all of the clips and sandwich the photograph between the back and the glass. It doesn't matter if the picture is too small for the frame. Use plain brown parcel tape to create a frame around your photograph, sticking the tape onto the backing to hold everything together. Make your border as wide or thin as you like, by overlapping tape if necessary. The beauty of framing this way is that you can then use your stampers, or a pen if you have especially beautiful handwriting, to label the picture with where and when it was taken. It's so quick and easy to do that you can get loads of pictures done in one go and fill a wall or shelf. Simple, cheap, practical and stylish…any more boxes to tick?

Make sweet souvenirs from old holiday maps

This is a cute way to remember holidays. Just bring back a map of the area – as used and ragged as you like – and cut a shape out of it. The free maps that come with car hire or from the tourist office are ideal. Go for any shape you fancy – a star, square, circle, butterfly are all great. Cookie cutters are very handy to use as templates. Use a little double-sided tape to fix the cut-out to a paper or card background to fit your frame. Write the date – either on the paper, or the back of the frame – and hang. These look fantastic grouped together.

Beach treasure magnets

On the subject of holiday mementoes, another lovely way to remember a special vacation is to make fridge magnets from the treasure you've combed from the beach.– one of my favourite holiday pastimes. I love nothing better than to trawl along the sand aimlessly, collecting pretty shells, stones, coral and driftwood as I go, my head completely empty as I scan for treasure. The little pieces look really pretty in a simple glass jar when you get back home – maybe with a tea light perched on top. But why not pick out the prettiest pieces and glue little magnets on the back so that they can be stuck on the fridge to hold photographs or notes. So sweet. (See these in action on my fridge on page 33.)

A cute and stylish way to remember holidays is to make sweet souvenirs from old holiday maps.

Simple

PLEASURES

HOMEMADE FIRESTARTERS

Whether you're camping, building a bonfire or are lucky enough to have an open fire at home, here is a fabulous old-fashioned way of making firelighters. This is a really satisfying way of turning something destined for the rubbish into something that works brilliantly, saves you money and is enjoyable to do. When you've finished reading the newspaper, simply pull the pages apart and take a single sheet. Fold it in half widthways. Keep doubling the paper in half until you have a long strip about 2cm wide. Fold it in half lengthways, twist the halves together and knot. There is something very therapeutic about sitting in companionable silence with your children, partner, whoever you can rope in, quietly twisting the papers into small, pleasing bundles. Pile them high in a basket by the fireplace. For a pile of rubbish, they actually look pretty stylish in an eco-chic way, and the tightly packed rolls burn slowly to get a really great fire going – just add some kindling and logs. Super satisfying.

THE FINEST MARSHMALLOW TOASTING FORKS EVER

For a child, toasting a marshmallow over an open fire is bliss. Taking care not to turn the outside black...the anticipation while waiting for it to cool... and finally the taste of the crisp sweet shell yielding to soft gooey inside. Heaven. It's not a bad treat for an adult either. At home, out barbecuing or camping, it's one of life's truly simple pleasures. Happily, the best thing to use as a toasting fork is a metal coat hanger. Just pull the bottom away from the top (the bit the trousers would fold over) and stretch so that the shape changes to an elongated diamond. This becomes the handle. Then stretch out the curled-over metal at the top (the bit that hangs on the rail), so that it is almost straight. This is where the marshmallows will get skewered. That's it. Genius. The finest toasting fork ever – and completely free. Pleasing in so many ways.

A BATH REST

As with all the best things in life, this is so simple, but I guarantee it will become one of the favourite things in your house because it makes taking a bath a luxurious, relaxing, spa-style indulgence. All you need is a piece of wood, measuring approximately 25 x 80 x 2.5cm. It should be deep enough to hold a couple of candles, a cup of tea – or a glass of wine – a book or magazines and a towel. The width might vary depending on your bath. Mine's a pretty bog-standard size, so 80cm spans it perfectly, but do measure the width of your bath to be sure your wood will be long enough. Look up a local timber yard and get them to cut a piece of wood to your dimensions. As it's a small piece they may well be able to do it from an off-cut, which will make it cheaper. If you don't mind the type of wood, just ask what's available. To finish it off, gently sand the edges to make sure it is totally smooth and then oil the wood to make it waterproof. The best oil is tung oil, which you can buy from the timber merchants. It is very thick, so dilute slightly with white spirit – you want it to be the consistency of olive oil. Wipe a thin coat over the wood. Leave for eight hours then do a second coat. Leave for another eight hours to soak in fully. If you apply the oil too liberally you will end up with a sticky finish because it won't absorb properly, so do be sparing.

Add bath oil, candles and a book for the perfect way to wind down at the end of another hard day!

Flowers
AND PLANTS

As a general rule, I opt for bulbs or plants over cut flowers, for two reasons: they last for ages and require very little maintenance once planted, so fulfill the wonderwoman mantra – 'minimum effort, maximum return' – but equally, there is something eminently stylish about a beautifully planted little container. However, if you want full on pretty, it has to be cut flowers.

MAKE CUT FLOWERS LAST

The best tip I have come across for making flowers last is a very simple one – don't ram them into a vase or pot that is too small, because it crushes the stems together and hampers them from taking up water freely. Obvious really. A stylish way to achieve this is to separate the stems into different jam jars and group them together, or line them up down the centre of a table or along a mantelpiece or shelf. I like the basic utilitarian look of the glass jars unadorned, but if you'd prefer something a little posher, you could tie the jars together with string or an elastic band and wrap a wide band of fabric around. Secure with a safety pin where you won't see it, or hide the pin with a ribbon tied around the fabric.

I haven't found that adding bicarb, charcoal or anything else to the water helps the longevity of the flowers, but changing the water every few days to keep it fresh does – clean the stems under running water at the same time. Also, when you are first arranging the flowers, strip the stems so that there are no leaves, which will just rot in the water. You don't need to worry about the sort of leaves that run the full length of the plant – as with hyacinths and tulips. Otherwise, do strip all the leaves off. Apart from

anything, I think the flowers look much prettier that way – uncluttered.

Get maximum life out of the flowers by cutting away the bottom of the stem as it starts to decompose, which prevents it properly absorbing water. Do this in small increments every four days or so, and cut at a slight angle, so the stem isn't flat against the bottom of the jar, which stops it being able to take up the water properly – think what happens to a straw when it's flat in the bottom of a glass. As the stems get ever shorter transfer the flowers to smaller containers.

HOW TO PLANT A CONTAINER

All you need to know here is that there are no rules. You can use absolutely any container you fancy – a cooking bowl, a metal pot, a wine crate, a teacup, a basket... really anything you have to hand that takes your fancy. If you are using something that is not watertight, line it first with a bin bag. Cut a piece of bin liner so that it will be big enough to come to the top of the container. You can trim it once you've added the soil, so that you don't see it. Next put a layer of potting soil in the bottom of the container, as high as you need it to be so that the bulbs or plants will sit at the right level – near the top, but low enough to be covered with another layer of soil. Put in your bulbs/plants, cover over with extra soil and pat down firmly. A stylish way to finish this off is to cover over the soil with some moss if you can get hold of it (for this reason I never try to kill off moss in my garden because I love making use of it). Don't forget to keep the container watered, so that the soil is always moist, but not waterlogged.If you've used a big container, add a layer of broken crockery or stones in with the soil, to help with drainage.

Wonder Tip

A good way to keep indoor plants hydrated is to spray them with a mist of water every day.

HERE ARE SOME OF THE BEST CONTAINER BULBS:
- **Lily of the valley**
- **Hyacinth**
- **Grape hyacinth**
- **Daffodil**
- **Snowdrop**

Don't worry that they will start life in your container as a very unassuming bulb. The anticipation of what is to come is part of the pleasure.

CREATE A FLOWER-STREWN LAWN

A magical way of getting maximum impact from bulbs is to spend a few hours on an autumn day dotting the lawn with bulbs. Use an old knife (a butter knife or similar) to pierce holes in the lawn. Wiggle it around to make an opening large enough for the bulb you're planting. Then press the ground back over the hole. Either go for one type or a mix – whatever you fancy. Plant as many as you can bear. Then forget all about it until the spring when, one day, with pride, you will notice the flowers starting to peep out of the lawn. A little effort you'd forgotten all about starting to pay off. And it will reward you every year as the bulbs divide and spread, multiplying the number of flowers each time they come, with zero input from you. Magic.

PLANT A BLOSSOM TREE

Why not just go the whole hog and plant a blossom tree somewhere you can see easily as you come home or out of the window. Buy something small and every year, as you watch it grow, it will be an amazing source of pleasure and pride as its beautiful blossom multiplies each spring, and you think, 'I did that!'.

Don't forget: Planters make great gifts –
just add a ribbon and a hand – printed label.

Homemade
PRESENTS AND ACTIVITIES

TOO OFTEN WE EQUATE money spent with sentiment expressed – the more valuable a gift, the more it means. How often do you find yourself desperately trying to think of something to buy for someone, when they really don't actually NEED anything. Similarly, we spend money on children, trying to assuage the guilt we feel about not always spending enough time with them. In fact, the gifts that are remembered, are the thoughtful ones, not neccessarily the most lavish. And quality time spent having fun with children will be remembered long after a toy has been tossed aside. So here are some simple, but thoughtful things to make for others, and fun but easy things to make and do with children.

Gift
IDEAS

Cinnamon sugar

Cinnamon has to be one of the most comforting tastes in the world. For some reason, buying cinnamon sugar is expensive, which is crazy because you can make your own very cheaply, in seconds, and it looks and tastes divine. All you need is a clean preserving jar, some unrefined caster sugar and ground cinnamon. Mix ½ teaspoon ground cinnamon per 100g of caster sugar. Make up as much as you need to fill your jar (i.e. 500g sugar plus 2½ teaspoons cinnamon). Do taste it and add a little more cinnamon if you want it stronger. Tuck a cinnamon stick into the jar if you want – but it's really for show more than anything. Heaven on a plate has to be this on some French toast... so while we're on the subject, here's how to make heavenly Pain Perdu – that's French for French toast!

Pain perdu

To feed 5 hungry mouths for breakfast. Whisk up 3 eggs, 150ml double cream, 50ml milk, 1 teaspoon vanilla essence and a pinch of salt. Dip sliced brioche into the mix, dunk well and put each slice on a sheet of baking paper, ready to be fried. Melt 25g of unsalted butter in a heavy frying pan. Brown the slices of brioche on both sides in the pan and serve. Crisp on the outside, meltingly fluffy within. Sprinkle over cinnamon sugar and serve with strawberries and blueberries or sliced apples.

As a gift, give a jar of sugar with a pretty vintage spoon attached, plus a handwritten label with the recipe for Pain Perdu.

Really yummy chocolate truffles

Super easy to make, and seriously, who doesn't love them? The following quantities will make about 30 truffles. Whip up 200ml of double cream, so that it is just getting thick and unctuous. Melt 200g of good dark chocolate (or a mix of dark and milk if you want less rich truffles) in the microwave. (Heat in 40-second bursts, stirring well between each blast, so that you don't risk overheating, which makes the chocolate go grainy). Let the chocolate cool a little and then pour it into the cream, stirring as you go. Add a good pinch of salt too – it really enhances the chocolate. If you have an electric mixer, it might be a good idea to deploy it here, because the mix will get very stiff, so you need to be quite strong for this if you're doing it by hand!

When the mix is ready, refrigerate in the bowl for about half an hour – it will be easier to form into balls when it's cold and firm. Meanwhile, put 3 or 4 tablespoons of cocoa powder in a bowl, ready to coat the truffles. To form the truffles, scoop out a generous teaspoon of the cold ganache and drop it into the bowl of cocoa powder by using a second teaspoon to scrape it off the spoon. Roll it around in the powder. When you've done about six, remove each, one by one and roll it around in your hands to make a ball. Once the shape's good, drop back into the cocoa powder to re-coat and transfer to a tray or plate covered with non-stick baking paper. Continue until you've used up all the mix. Refrigerate again.

When they've set, transfer to a gift bag, box or jar, attach a ribbon, and a note to say they should be kept refrigerated, but eaten at room temperature. They will keep for about five days – if they last that long!

SALTED CARAMELISED NUTS

These are heavenly and make for a really indulgent treat, or a great gift for someone. And they are incredibly easy to make.

YOU NEED:
- **40g unsalted butter**
- **200g caster sugar**
- **150g almonds**
- **150g pecans**
- **generous pinch of salt**

Before you start cooking, put a piece of non-stick baking paper on the side, ready for the nuts. Melt the butter in a heavy frying pan, then add the sugar and salt. Once the sugar starts to catch, stir vigorously and constantly so the heat is spread evenly and you don't get burnt spots. When the sugar is completely molten and a rich dark caramel colour, add the nuts. Stir around to ensure all the nuts are coated. Transfer to the non-stick paper. Spread out using a spatula. Don't touch with your fingers, as the sugar is boiling hot. Leave to cool. It doesn't matter if there are big clumps – you can break them up more when they are cold. Wait until the nuts are completely cold, then put in a preserving jar to store, or give away. I guarantee that anyone who tastes these will ask you for the recipe!

FABULOUS FAIRY WINGS

Which little girl doesn't love to scamper around in fairy wings? And frankly, which mother doesn't love to admire her dinky little daughter looking like an angel – even if she doesn't always behave like one? These are the most beautiful wings, and they are so easy to make, and will cost you nothing!

All you need are a couple of metal coat hangers, some tape, some elastic, some ribbon, an old pair of tan tights, some gold spray paint, some glue and some glitter. First, cut the hanging loops off the hangers using a set of pliers. Then pull each hanger open, so that it looks like a wing. Place them next to each other so that the necks of the hangers are overlapping. Secure them firmly together with parcel tape. It doesn't matter how ugly the tape looks, as it will be covered, but you want to make sure the two pieces are stuck together well.

Now cut at the knee of each leg of the tights. Stretch a leg over each wing, so that the toe is over the outer edge and the raw edge is at the centre of the wings, where you have taped them together. Make sure the fabric is pulled tight, and secure firmly in the middle with more tape. Now spray-paint the wings gold. Once they are dry, paint patterns on the wings with glue, and sprinkle glitter over. Again, leave to dry. Make straps to attach the wings under the child's armpits. You need two 40cm lengths of 1cm-width elastic. Tie to form two bands. Wind ribbon around the middle section, securing with double-sided tape. Loop the bands over the wings onto the middle section. Done!

A FABULOUS FAIRY SKIRT

This couldn't be simpler to make, but it is so effective and any little girl would love it. All you need is material, some elastic, netting and ribbon. Cut a piece of fabric to make the waistband, measuring 6 x 140cm (or the full width of a piece of fabric). Fold it in half and iron, then fold each edge under by 1cm to make a seam, and iron again. Now cut three strips of netting measuring 15 x 140cm, 20 x 140cm and 25 x 140cm. Lay these on top of each other – longest piece first – and pin to the inside of the waist band. Cut strips of ribbon 25cm long and pin those on top of the netting. Now machine stitch along the length of the waistband to secure the netting and ribbon to it. Fold the band over and stitch, to make a channel. Thread the elastic through, pull to fit your child and knot. Very basic but very gorgeous.

Check out the homemade leggings! See page 120 for how easy these are to make.

149

A CHILD'S STYLISH WORK OF ART

As children get older and produce lovely pictures, framing them makes perfect gifts for parents and grandparents. A good way of making a great gift from a little one's paint splodges or scribbles is to cut a shape out of it and frame.

AN EXTRA-SPECIAL FRAMED PHOTOGRAPH

I absolutely love this! It's an amazingly simple but effective way of framing a picture to make it even more beautiful and special as a gift. Just put a layer of fabric between the glass and the photograph with a shape cut out of it. You want a fairly thick fabric so that the rest of the photograph can't be seen underneath the material. Cut a piece of fabric to size by removing the glass from the frame, drawing around it and then cutting out your rectangle. Cookie cutters are the easiest templates to use for the shape that you want to cut out. Select one that will be a good size for the area of the photograph you want to show. Draw around it on the fabric and cut out the shape. A heart is perfect because it is very easy to cut. Just fold the fabric in half, with the fold running down the centre line of the heart, and cut along the ear-shaped line. When you unfold the fabric, the heart will be complete. Rub along the rough edges of the fabric so that it frays slightly, and trim away any straggly threads. Position the fabric over the photograph and frame. Simple, speedy and super effective.

WEDDING GIFT PHOTOGRAPH

This is an uber version of the simple fabric frame that would make a really thoughtful and special wedding gift. An effective alternative and pertinent cut-out would be a traditional wedding cake design, which is really easy to do – just sketch the shape onto the fabric and cut out. Use a ballpoint pen to write the couple's initials, plus the wedding date, on the fabric. Sew over the pen lines, to embroider the details, with a simple continuous running stitch.

A CHARM BRACELET

To make a special occasion charm bracelet as a present, follow the instructions in the 'Things to Make with Kids' section, page 158, but weave little charms into the bracelet as you go. You can buy vintage silver charms very cheaply online or at markets. Little engraved silver discs work really well too.

BOOKMARK WITH A FAVOURITE QUOTE

Stampers and ink work brilliantly on heavy fabric, like linen or thick cotton. A great way to combine the two is to make little bookmarks with quotes. Just cut out a piece of plain linen, or heavy cotton, measuring 20 x 5cm. Use regular scissors and then machine stitch a hemline around the sides about 0.5cm in to stop the edges fraying, or else cut with pinking shears. Then stamp out your quote (make sure it's not too long and that it will fit), which obviously can be pertinent to the occasion, if you're giving it as a present.

Cards

I love making cards. It takes very little effort, but a small burst of creativity is always satisfying. There's no limit to what you can do, especially if you've got a printer. Print photographs or other images directly onto art card. Cut out shapes or letters from patterned paper, fabric or lace – use a cookie cutter if you're uncertain about drawing the shape yourself. Print out a favourite poem and cut a shape out of it – it doesn't matter that the words are incomplete.

Or you could draw a heart and write a poem or passage inside it, with the words weaving around the shape and spiralling into the centre. You could stamp out a quote on the front of the card. Another really funky idea is to cut out letters from a newspaper or magazine to spell out a greeting, or numbers for an age card, and then overstamp with little butterfly or other shaped stampers. I also love using my label maker to type out plastic strips with greetings. Or I borrow my daughter's badge-maker and make a badge for the front of the card. My current favourite is printing with potato stampers (see page 159) – the options are endless!

Buying cards can be ridiculously expensive, especially if you go for the ones that look vaguely hand-made. Yours will look infinitely nicer and cost infinitely less. If you keep a stock of art card you will always have the wherewithal to make and send a stylish card for any occasion.

Wrap

Armed with a roll of kraft paper, some stampers and inks or paints, you can wrap presents beautifully and cheaply. There are two ways to do this. First up, the lazy way, because that is my preferred option – naturally. Wrap the gift in plain brown paper, and then dot your stampers all over it to prettify. This works brilliantly if you have wrapped a book, or something else that will hold firm against the stamp as you press it down.

If you have wrapped something really soft – like an item of clothing – the stamper won't make its mark properly, because the paper will yield too much. In that case, cut out paper to the size you need, and stamp it before wrapping. Let the ink dry before wrapping, so that it doesn't smudge. Leave the present as it is, or tie string, ribbon or a strip of fabric around. Either stamp or write who the gift is to and from directly onto the parcel, or make a little tag from a square (or any other shape) of card, punch a hole though and attach. Isn't it so much nicer to give – and receive – a beautifully wrapped present?

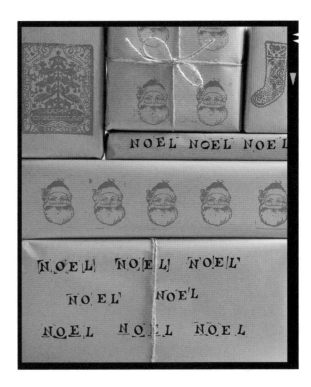

A DOLL'S HOUSE OUT OF OLD WINE CASES

Most wine comes in cardboard boxes, but good bottles are still supplied to merchants in stylish wooden crates that are just begging to be reused. Shops are normally very happy to give them away, if you just ask. Sometimes I strike lucky and get several in exchange for a donation into the charity box, but other times they don't have any – just pop in when you're passing. Here's just one simple but brilliant way to transform them.

This doll's house is made from three wine cases, which form a basic structure that can be left plain or decorated as elaborately as you want it to be. As you can see in the picture, two cases stuck together form each half of the house; the third provides planks for room dividers and the roof. Once you've made the house, it's great fun to rope in the children so you can decorate it together.

First, remove any protruding metal pins from two boxes. This is easily done with a screwdriver, which can be jimmied under any tight pins to work them out of the wood, and a pair of pliers. Glue the boxes together with strong wood glue. Completely pull apart the third wine case. Use your screwdriver to prise the sides away from the base and pull them apart, so that you end up with five separate pieces of wood. Remove any nails or staples that are in the wood. The two smaller end pieces of the case will become the ceiling of the ground floor/floor of the top floor – just apply glue around the back and sides to fix them firmly into place.

Now you can make the roof with the two longer narrow pieces. The easiest way to do this is by using parcel tape to stick the pieces together at the point that will form the apex of the roof and then placing it in position on top of the main structure. Attach the base of the roof to the top of the house with more parcel tape. I like the look of this as it is – plain and simple, with little cut-out images from magazines: a bath, oven, chandeliers, paintings, fireplace – but if you wanted you could wallpaper it and even stick bits of carpet on the floor. It's so much fun making and decorating this cute little house – you'll feel like a child again! And your kids will love it! And it's free! If you don't have children, or yours are too old for this, why not make one as a gift for someone else. I promise you will love making it.

A WINE-CRATE TOY BOX

This is a lovely way to store a child's special toys – like a little tea set or dolls – and is a really special way to package up something as a present. Measure the bottom and sides of the box and cut paper to fit – it's easiest to cut five separate pieces. Fix double-sided adhesive tape around the four sides of each rectangle. Check each piece of paper fits before you stick it on. Then, starting with the base, remove the protective layer from the tape, so that you can stick the paper to it. Do the same with each of the sides. Decorate the outside of the box with the child's name and stampers. So cute.

With a little imagination you can turn old wine crates into something really special.

Things to Make

SALT DOUGH FRIDGE MAGNETS

Salt dough is so easy to make and it's a great thing to do with kids because there are so many things you can create with it. One of the simplest and most useful is fridge magnets.

YOU WILL NEED:
- **1 cup plain flour**
- **½ cup table salt**
- **½ cup water**
- **1 tbsp lemon juice**

(this makes the dough set really hard)

The children can do the mixing by hand, or you can combine everything in the mixer. You want a smooth dough that holds well together. If it's sticky, add a little extra flour. If it's too dry, add a little extra water. Give each child a piece of non-stick baking paper, a lump of dough, and a rolling pin and let them roll it out (2–3mm thickness is perfect). Then get a range of cutters for them to stamp out their shapes. You can leave the shapes to dry out naturally, which will take a couple of days, or bake them on the lowest heat in the oven for a few hours. If you want to leave them plain, air-drying is best because they dry to a beautiful crisp white. If they will be painted and decorated, drying out in the oven is fine. It will slightly discolour them and change the texture a little. Once the shapes are finished, stick little magnetic discs on the back (which you can easily buy online), put on the fridge and let the children admire.

> ### Wonder Tip
> Imprint patterns onto the salt dough using Indian printing blocks for a really stylish touch.

PLAYDOUGH

Playdough is one of those things that kids love and we hate, because it gets everywhere and is a nightmare to clear up. There are two options here – ban the stuff, or else make a quick, cheap and easy version that can be binned without guilt.

YOU WILL NEED:
- **1 cup plain flour**
- **1 cup boiling water**
- **few drops of food colouring**
- **½ cup salt**
- **2 tbsp oil (any sort)**
- **glitter**

Put everything except the glitter into a mixing bowl and stir well – or else use the electric mixer to make it even quicker and easier. When the dough is starting to come together, add in 2 tbsp glitter and continue to mix. The dough is ready when it comes together in a ball. If it's too sticky, add more flour. If it's too dry, add more water. Lay some greaseproof paper on the table, plus cookie cutters, rolling pins, an old garlic press (makes brilliant hair) and anything else that they can use to shape and primp their playdough and let them go crazy.

Snow globes

These are fabulous to make with children, on a rainy day, or to entertain a bigger crowd for a party.

YOU WILL NEED:
- **One jam jar per child**
- **Small plastic toy/animal/character to stick inside**
- **Glitter/sparkles**
- **Waterproof craft glue**
- **Glycerin**
- **Distilled water** (This is to give the snow globe longevity – ordinary tap water will discolour over time. Buy from a hardware store.)

Let each child choose a figure, then help them glue it to the underside of the jam-jar lid. This now has to be left until the glue has set completely hard. (Now might be a good time to put on a movie or go out and play for a bit!) Pour water into the glass jar so that it is about three quarters full. Add a few drops of glycerin. This is to make the water slightly viscous so that the 'snow' doesn't just fall to the bottom of the globe instantly after it's been shaken. Then add about half a teaspoon of sprinkles or glitter to the water. Add more water, so the jar is filled right up to the top. Once you're sure the figure is securely anchored to the lid/base, screw the lid on. Turn over and admire the snow globe in action!

LET THE KIDS MAKE JELLY

It's a good discipline to be able to hold back and let little ones get on with doing things for themselves, but it can go against all our instincts – particularly when you're thinking about the cleaning up you'll have to do afterwards. Jelly is the perfect thing for this, because it's so easy, they really can't go wrong. Let the children make it while you hide in the background, giving them confidence to do something without your constant supervision.

THE YUMMIEST AND EASIEST CHOCOLATE AND NUT COOKIES IN THE WORLD

Cooking with the kids is one of my favourite things to do on a lazy Saturday morning when it's wet and dull outside. And what could be better than making cookies to have with milk for elevenses cuddled up in front of a movie?

YOU WILL NEED:
- 250g unsalted butter
- 350g soft brown sugar
- 1 large egg
- 400g plain flour
- 1 tsp vanilla extract
- pinch of salt
- 150g milk or plain chocolate, or malt balls covered in chocolate, chopped into small chunks
- 100g pecans/walnuts chopped into small chunks

Pre-heat the oven to 180°C. Put everything in the mixer except the chocolate and nuts. If the butter is straight out of the fridge – and mine always is because I'm never organised enough to get it out early – just squish it into small pieces with your hands (or better still let hot eager little hands do it) as it goes into the bowl.

Mix until everything has come together to form a soft but firm cookie dough. This may take ten minutes if the butter was cold. Then add the chocolate and nuts and mix again so they are evenly distributed through the dough. At this stage it's a good idea to refrigerate the dough for about fifteen minutes, if you can bear it. This stops the dough spreading during cooking. It's not vital, and depends on how hungry you are! Line two baking trays with a sheet of non-stick paper. Roll mix into walnut sized balls and press down on the paper. Cook for fifteen minutes. Leave to cool, then eat!

Alternative: Stud Smarties into the top of the cookies instead of mixing in chocolate and nuts.

TIP: This makes a lovely gift idea too. Just layer the dried ingredients into a large jar. Put the nuts and chocolate into a separate bag and attach. Add a ribbon and a handprinted label, plus recipe instructions.

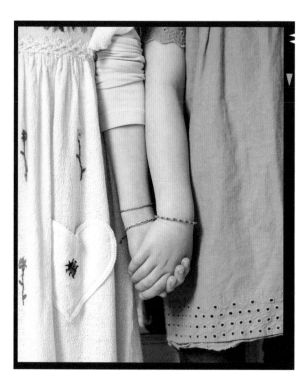

string. Let go. Now pick up the left-hand string, knot twice over the middle string and then twice again over the right-hand string. Repeat over and again until you have a knotted bracelet that will span the wearer's wrist. Knot the threads together and then plait for 4cm. Finally, tie another knot. Trim the ends to neaten.

SUPER-EASY FRIENDSHIP BRACELETS

This super-simple version is probably better for children under nine, because the previous version does require quite a lot of manual dexterity. For this one, the children can just plait the strings. They can jazz them up by threading on beads or little charms.

Alternatively, plait strips of fabric instead of thread for a chunky, funky look.

MAKE GARLANDS FROM CHILDREN'S PICTURES

A double bonus, because this isn't just something to do with children, but something to do with the acres of artwork they produce. As they get older, it's nice to keep a file of their best pictures, but when they're little, they can be pretty prolific with paint daubed on paper – you feel guilty throwing it away (especially when they peer into the bin and spot it), but if you don't, you get swamped. A great solution is to make garlands from the pictures. Cut out circles and machine stitch them together, buttressed against each other, to form a continuous chain of discs. The children can trace around shapes and practise their scissor skills by cutting around the outlines. If you don't have a sewing machine, use a needle and thread and do a simple running stitch through each piece. Hang the colourful garland up in their bedroom for them to admire.

FRIENDSHIP BRACELETS

I used to love making these when I was young, and still love making them now. It's a great thing to do with children because they are very simple to make, and it's soooo satisfying to see how a series of basic little knots can create something so pretty. The children will love to make them for their friends too. All you need is some string. Cut three 75cm lengths of thread, either all the same colour or different, depending on whether you want a plain or striped bracelet. Knot the strands together at one end, and tape the raw ends to a tabletop, to hold it firm as you work. Plait the strands together in a simple braid for about 4cm. Tie another knot. Now take the string on the left-hand side and knot it twice over the centre string. Knot the same string twice over the right-hand

POTATO PRINTING ON CLOTHES

Potato printing is one of my favourite things because it is so basic, but effective. Just cut a potato in half and press a cookie cutter deep into the flesh. Cut away around the edge using a sharp knife. Now just add fabric paint and get stamping.

unused until you can be bothered to empty it out. When you finally do there's a large circular patch of dead lawn. And then how do you dry the deflated and wizened plastic before you put it away? Inevitably there'll be loads of wrinkles where water lurks, so when you get it out next summer it's got green sludgy bits all over it. So you throw it away. But then in a moment of amnesia, you buy another one. And so the cycle goes on. So really, forget a paddling pool. The best, best, best thing is the good old sprinkler. I love the nostalgia of it all, transporting me back to the long, hot summers of my childhood. Most of all, I love the simplicity of it. Too often we make things harder for ourselves when it really isn't worth it.

HAVE A WATER FIGHT

One of life's simplest pleasures, and the most fun way to cool down on a boiling hot summer's day. You don't need water pistols – old squeezy ketchup or washing-up bottles are perfect. Just fill and squirt. This is a fabulously cheap way to keep the kids entertained – they'll play for hours outside – but don't forget to join in yourself sometimes too, and feel the years roll away as you're transported back to the blissful simplicity of childhood.

FLIP CARTOONS

All you need are little plain notepads – one per child – plus a pencil and colouring pencils/crayons per child. Show them how they can build up a flash cartoon strip by drawing something simple like a stick man on each page and making it different each time, so that when the pages are flicked together, the stick man runs, or dances, or a car drives across the page, or Superman flies, or Spiderman spins a web, a ballerina

TURN ON THE SPRINKLER

A sprinkler is just soooo much easier and more fun than a paddling pool. The thing is, on the first hot day of the year the idea of the pool is hard to resist. You've forgotten how long it takes to blow up and then fill up. And how the kids won't get in because the water's too cold, so you have to traipse back and forth to the kitchen boiling the kettle over and over until the icy edge is taken off. Then there is a brief moment of bliss when the kids will splash around for a while and summer has really arrived. The problem is, when they're done for the day, you can't face the thought of emptying out the water and starting all over again tomorrow, so you just it in leave in. Then the next day the children complain there are bugs in it. Which there are. And slimy leaves. So they won't get in, and the pool lurks there for a few more days dances, or a flower bends in the wind. The children absolutely love doing this and it can go on for ages, depending on how intricate their little drawings are. It can be an ongoing project that they keep returning to until the little book is completely filled.

How about doing a
SKILLS SWAP WITH A FRIEND

Sometimes it's easier to have more children around – often yours will play much better when they've got their friends. Why not take this one step further? Get together with a friend and take all her kids for an afternoon to do an activity you enjoy – like cooking, for instance. Then she can take yours the next week to teach them something she's good at – like sewing, for instance. This way, the kids are happy – they get to do something fun with their friends – and you get a whole afternoon off. Obviously, you double the number of kids in your care for the return fixture, but as I say, more really can be easier.

Play the Shape Game

I was introduced to this by the children's author Anthony Browne. He is absolutely passionate about fostering imagination and creativity in kids, and this is a brilliant way to do it. Basically, one person draws a shape – any shape, crazy or simple. Then the other person has to turn the shape into a picture. This is a great thing to do on a rainy day – it can go on for hours. It also works brilliantly for a party. Just stick a giant piece of paper onto a wall and get the kids to take it in turns to draw the shape and turn it into a picture.

Play the chocolate game

A roast for Sunday lunch, a brisk walk and then a great old-fashioned children's game. Are there many more blissful, carefree ways to spend a day? Just in case you've forgotten how to play this old favourite, you'll need a bar of chocolate, a knife and fork, a dice and a scarf, hat and pair of gloves. Each person takes it in turns to roll the dice. When someone lands a six they must quickly put on the winter woollies and use the knife and fork to cut up and eat the chocolate. Everyone else carries on throwing the dice. As soon as another six is thrown, the hat, scarf and gloves have to be removed and passed on, etc, etc.

Special
OCCASIONS

HOW OFTEN have you been looking forward to a

big event like a birthday party or Christmas, only to

not really enjoy it because you're too stressed to relax?

Too often we pile on the pressure in our desire to make

sure everything is perfect and forget what is actually

important - enjoying time together with loved ones.

So think smart and cut corners where you can. You want

to invest your effort where you'll get maximum return.

This chapter is about helping you strike the balance.

Children's
BIRTHDAY PARTIES

All of the ideas for things to do with kids on previous pages can very easily be used to occupy and entertain children at a party. They also mean the kids make their own take-home present, which saves you the job of doing party bags – major bonus! Supplement an arty activity, with some party games or a movie plus tea, and you've got a great kids' party.

Come up with a list of party games by channelling memories of your own childhood – remember the games that gave you simple pleasure when you were young. To get you inspired, here's my list:

- **Pass the parcel**
- **Pin the tail on the donkey**
- **Musical statues**
- **Musical bumps**
- **What's the time Mr Wolf?**
- **The hokey-cokey**
- **Potato and spoon relay races**
- **Simon says**
- **Musical chairs**
- **Treasure hunts** – Divide the children up into small teams. Each team has a colour. Hide colour-coded envelopes in different locations with clues in them that will lead each team onto the next clue. Start by handing each team their first clue, and then hide up to eight more envelopes for each. Hide prizes for each team at the final destination.
- **Charades**
- **Karaoke**
- **A movie, plus popcorn**

Don't forget to rope in other adults. Magic tricks, performed by a dad or an uncle, with little or no skill, are always good. One of our biggest party hits was to get a dad to dress up as Father Christmas to hand out party presents at the end of a pre–Christmas birthday celebration. Completely free, but it was magical. If you've got older children, don't forget to use them and their friends as a source of free labour – they love to get involved. Otherwise, find out which mums are planning to stay for the party – or ask one or two to do so, and offer to return the favour for them – and ask them to muck in with supervising and helping serve tea.

The wonderwoman's greatest trick is knowing when it's worth putting in extra effort and when to make no effort at all. Birthday party food is a perfect example of this. There really is no point spending ages producing a fabulous party feast, because invariably the kids are too excited to eat much and besides, all they want to consume is the staple party junk food, like crisps, biscuits and cocktail sausages, that you can produce with barely any effort at all. So, don't stress on that front. There is, however, one element of the food where it is worth investing some effort – the birthday cake. Kids seem to remember the specific details of every birthday cake they have ever been served. It is the totemic moment of a party – the ceremony of it, with the candles burning and everyone joining in to sing happy birthday. So, allow me to introduce...

As with so many things, when it comes to children's party games, the old'uns are the gold'uns!

The

ULTIMATE CAKE

THE ULTIMATE CAKE

This is a cake you must make once in your life if you have a daughter. I was prompted to do it by my then two-year-old, who spotted the most magnificently outrageous cake in the window of a Chinese bakery and hankered after it from that moment. It was enormous and beautiful. This is my scaled-down version, but it still provoked gasps of delight from my three daughters and their assembled friends.

To make it, you will first need to locate a Barbie – or similar – doll. To prepare the doll (and I'm afraid this feels horribly weird and brutal), you need to snap off her legs, so that she will sit neatly on top of her skirt. Next, style her hair. There is a practical reason for this: you don't want your beautiful creation to go down in flames if one of the birthday candles catches hold of her ultra-flammable locks. So cut her hair to shoulder length and then pull it up into a very high ponytail. Now leave her to one side and crack on with the cake.

I maybe should have mentioned earlier, the reason this is a do-once-in-a-lifetime job, is that it will take you several hours to make, because you need three separate sponge cakes to sandwich together. However, the reward and satisfaction reaped from making it still fits with the bottom line that reward must outweigh the effort it takes. And in spite of the time it entails, it is not difficult – no special skill required. OK…

YOU WILL NEED:

For the sponge:
(total required for three layers to make one cake)
- **390g self-raising flour**
- **390g caster sugar**
- **390g butter**
- **90ml milk (at room temperature)**
- **6 eggs (at room temperature)**
- **1½ teaspoons vanilla extract**
- **pinch of salt**

For the icing:
- **500g icing sugar**
- **160g unsalted butter**
- **50ml milk**
- **½ teaspoon vanilla extract**
- **pink food colouring**
(assuming you want a pink dress)

For the filling:
- **1 big bag marshmallows**

- **glitter and decorations galore**
- **board to put the cake on** (a chopping board – covered with foil if you want – will suffice)
- **3 cake tins,** around 20–22cm square or in diameter.

Please don't be daunted by the recipe overleaf. Go for it!

THE ULTIMATE CAKE RECIPE

Use whatever tins you have – square or round. It's great to use a slightly larger one for the bottom layer, if you have one. If not, you can shape the skirt with a knife when the pieces are all stacked together. Line the tins with non-stick baking paper. **Pre-heat the oven to 170°C**. Only cook one cake in the oven at a time. If you have a double oven, obviously two can be cooked simultaneously. If you can cook two tins at once, prepare two thirds of the ingredients. If not, prepare one third and repeat three times.

Combine the flour, sugar, butter and salt in a bowl and mix well until it is like dough. If you are using an electric mixer, use the hook attachment. **In a separate bowl, whisk the eggs, milk and vanilla extract together.** Add to the flour mixture, combining initially with a fork. Mix together for about five minutes at high speed, until it is smooth and creamy. Pour into the tin/s and **cook for about twenty-five minutes**. Check at fifteen minutes. The cake is ready when the surface is risen and golden, and when you prod a finger on the dome and the indentation quickly bounces back. To be absolutely certain, stick a metal skewer (I keep a cut length from a wire coat hanger in a kitchen drawer for this purpose) into the centre of the cake. If it emerges completely clean, the cake is done. **Leave to cool.**

When all three cakes are made and cool, cut the domed surface off the two that will form the bottom layers. Place the largest (if you made one bigger than the others) on the cake board. Now for the fabulous filling – probably the finest birthday cake filling in the world – **the marshmallows. Put them in a clear microwaveable bowl and cook for about one minute.** They might not need that long. It's important that the bowl is see-through so that you can watch them through the glass door as they heat. They will suddenly swell and puff up like billowing clouds. Just as they are starting to meld together, they're ready. Take them out of the microwave and use a palette knife or spatula to smear half the bowl over the cake. **Note: It is vital the cake is completely cool at this stage so the marshmallow sits on top as a separate layer**. If the cake is still warm the marshmallow will just be absorbed into it. Sit the next layer on top and smear over the rest of the marshmallow before squidging the final cake layer on top. Leave to set for ten minutes or so. Then use a sharp knife to finesse the outline of the skirt. It does not need to be perfect, just not too angular. Cut a small semi-circle in the top of the cake to sit the doll's trunk in.

Next make the icing. The key to the lightest butter icing ever is to incorporate plenty of air into it. To that end, firstly, sieve the icing sugar. Add the soft butter, milk and vanilla to the icing sugar and use a wooden spoon to lightly combine. Basically you don't want to create a major dust cloud when the electric mixer starts up. Start the mixer on a slow speed and gradually turn up until you are at top speed. Leave it to mix for about two minutes. Turn it off. Scrape the sides and bottom of the bowl with a spatula to make sure it is all mixing uniformly. Add a little food colouring. (Start with a tiny amount – you can always add more). Then put the mixer back on maximum and whip the icing for at least five minutes more.

Next is the fun part – dressing the doll. **Use a blunt knife to cover her skirt and body with icing.** Decorate with whatever spangles, baubles and glitter you can muster. (If you're using silver balls, stick them on using tweezers.) Stand back and admire.

LESS OUTRAGEOUS, BUT STILL FABULOUS

Using little plastic toys and characters is a really easy way of making a cake look fantastic. For a boy's birthday I would do a double-layer square cake (i.e. two thirds of the quantities opposite) and colour the icing an appropriate hue to match the theme, then pile on their favourite characters. So green icing, plus plastic dinosaurs rampaging all over it. Or, ice with plain frosting and then make up a runny black icing, and draw a giant spider's web over the surface. Now perch Spiderman on top. You could also use a thicker black icing, piped from a thick plastic bag with a small hole cut in one corner, to draw train tracks all over the cake and then place toy trains on them. Or dye the icing blue for Batman. Or pink with Peppa Pig characters for a girl. Or my all-time simple favourite – use Smarties or another soft sweet and make patterns or just liberally dot them all over the cake.

THE DECORATIONS

For the same amount of money as you would spend on paper cloths, you can buy cheap fabric and 'make' tablecloths that can come out time and again. I say 'make' in inverted commas because literally all you need to do is cut lengths of fabric to cover the table. Obviously you want cheap fabric. My favourite option is a polycotton gingham because it looks stylish but bright, and the fabric doesn't need to be ironed, so you just wash, fold and store after each use. If you can't buy it locally, there are loads of outlets online. Use pinking shears to cut the ends and it won't fray – no sewing required. And, of course, bunting galore – so simple to make, and great for giving a room a party feel. See page 123 for details on how to make it. String fairy lights around the room and your party grotto will be complete. The beauty is, all of this stuff can be pulled out and reused for the next party, and the next, saving you time and money forever after. Also, it brings an element of continuity and tradition that children love.

A QUICK THOUGHT
ON YOUR OWN BIRTHDAY

Try to NEVER, EVER work on your birthday. Once you hit adulthood, it's easy to forget the magic of birthdays. I certainly did and was never bothered about working on mine. Until my eldest was five and she was utterly distraught that I was due to clock in as normal on my birthday. She couldn't understand why I didn't see what was wrong with it. Aghast, I managed to duck out of my shift. Not quite sure what to do with my new-found free time I went for a manicure and pedicure. The best of my life. The indulgence! I wandered around a beautiful perfume department for about an hour, sniffing everything, just revelling in not having to be anywhere else or do anything else. So on your birthday, give yourself the day off. I mean really off – no laundry or anything – and simply enjoy your day. If the children aren't at school and childcare is an issue, try to prevail on a friend or relative to look after them as a birthday present. You could offer to return the favour on their birthday.

PS Don't forget to
invite your mum and dad
nice and early!

Mother's day

AND FATHER'S DAY

MOTHER'S DAY

The idea of entertaining on a day when you're supposed to be putting your feet up is a tricky one. You could go out, but the problem with going to a restaurant on a day that everyone else is celebrating too is that a) you need to book fiendishly early to get a table, and b) you will be offered a cheeky set menu for an exorbitant price, because the restaurant will be trying to cash in on demand. I would suggest getting your partner to cook or opting for a slow roast – my favourite minimum effort, maximum return meal. Just whack it in the oven, forget about it, then claim the credit for a sumptuously tender offering.

Spend a bit of the time you've saved on cooking putting in a little effort to make the table look beautiful. Throw over a stylish linen cloth – simply a full-width length of fabric cut at each end with pinking shears to save hemming. You could make napkins in a contrasting colour – again just cut simple squares. A very pretty and striking way to put flowers on the table for Mother's Day is to put little plants in teacups and run them down the table, interspersed with tea lights. Tie ribbons on the back of chairs.

On the pudding front, simply wheel out a plain shop-bought cake and give it a makeover. Two suggestions that both look really beautiful: shake cocoa powder or icing sugar over the top of the cake using a sieve and then stud with fresh flowers. Or, place a doily on top of the cake, sprinkle cocoa powder or icing sugar over it, remove the doily, et voila! Add berries around the edges or on top. Let the compliments roll in, while you spend the time you've saved on real hard work enjoying the day and relaxing. Pah! Restaurant schmestaurant.

MOTHER'S DAY GIFT IDEAS

- **A home-made lavender bag**
- **a beautiful teacup and selection of teas**
- **a silver disc or heart** engraved with a thought or quote that she can slip round her wrist or key ring
- **a vintage brooch**
- **a book or movie you've loved**
- **lunch out with you**
- **a cooking lesson with you**
- **a day out with you**
- **a spa treatment**
- **a bookmark** (see page 150)
- **home-made face oil** and muslins wrapped prettily together with string
- **a home pedicure kit** with a fabulous selection of polishes
- **a magazine subscription.**

FATHER'S DAY GIFT IDEAS

- **Some one-on-one dad time** Take your dad out for lunch.
- **A bit of dad bonding.** Send the dads wine tasting or go-karting together
- **Tickets to a show or concert**

From the kids: • A glass jar filled with favourite sweets with 'to the greatest dad in the world', typed out on a plastic label maker and stuck on.
- **A t-shirt** with a picture by the children reproduced on the front (printer shops will do this pretty cheaply). Or with children's hand/footprints in fabric paint.
- **A photo concertina for his office**
- **A framed child's picture**

Valentine's
DAY

I'm never quite sure about Valentine's Day. When I was younger – much younger – at school – I loved the anticipation of the day. Would a secret admirer reveal a secret fondness for me? Unfortunately, reality always trumped fantasy, when other girls would show off the numerous cards they'd received, while I quietly pretended I wasn't bothered not to have any. Then, when you are in a relationship, you think why does this day – dictated to us by tradition – have to be the day when we show our love for each other? We tell it to each other every day. I'm probably weird, but I hate to be sent flowers on Valentine's Day, because I know they'll be twice as expensive as if they'd been sent a day sooner or later, but they don't mean any more. Romance, it seems to me, is more spontaneous – a night out, or a gift sprung unexpectedly, just because. However, assuming you can't quite bear to ignore Valentine's Day altogether, do use it as a reason to break the habit of supper on a tray in front of the TV, and sit down for a candle-lit meal. Actually being able to sit down together and chat properly over a meal can be a rare indulgence when the natural default when you're not working or kid-corralling is to collapse on the sofa. This is about spending time together, not getting over-stressed trying to produce restaurant-style food after the kids have gone to bed, so pull out of your wonderwoman armoury the...

...HEART–SHAPED PUDDING

A cheeky trick to add va va voom to a shop-bought pudding. All you need is a ready-made dessert (tarts and cakes work best) of your choice and a heart-shaped cookie cutter. Cut out a couple of hearts. Put each on a plate. Use a sieve to dust lightly with icing sugar or cocoa powder, put a few berries or caramelised nuts on the side and voila! A pudding that looks like you have lovingly slaved over it for hours. Minimum effort – maximum return!

DECORATE THE TABLE WITH...

...blackboard candle holders (see page 110) with love notes scribbled on, candles and tea lights galore. Don't forget the music – remember what you listened to when you were first together?

VALENTINE'S GIFTS
- **A basket of home-made cookies**
- **A linen bookmark** with a hand-printed romantic quote (see page 150)
- **A heart-shaped framed map** or special memento (see page 136)
- **A glass jar of lovehearts**
- **Tickets to somewhere or something**

There is something so pleasing about these beautiful, slightly kitsch paper shells.

Easter

TIME

Papier mâché eggs

I love, love, love papier mâché eggs – a stylish alternative to shop-bought chocolate ones. You can buy them ready-made and decorated – just search online for 'papier mâché (or cardboard) eggs' and you will find a treasure trove of new and vintage offerings. You can also buy unfinished papier mâché shells and decorate them yourself. Or you can go the whole hog, and make papier mâché eggs yourself. This requires more effort, obviously, but it's fun to do with the kids and they are very easy to make.

All you need are some balloons, some torn-up newspapers and some wallpaper glue. You probably remember doing this as a child, which is why making them is so pleasing – regressing to childhood can be very therapeutic. Blow up a regular-shaped balloon to the size you want your egg to be. Tie a knot. Mix up the wallpaper paste in a large bowl, according to the instructions on the packet. Layer strips of torn paper over the balloon, dipping each in the paste as you go, so that they are saturated with glue. Part of the pleasure here is getting your hands dirty and smearing the glue around liberally – it is so tactile! You do need to let the paper dry out between layers. The best way is to hang the eggs on a washing line – as long as it's a dry day. Otherwise, suspend a line indoors and peg the end of the balloon, where the knot is tied, onto the line. You need to build up at least three layers.

Once the eggs are dry, paint or decorate the outside of the shell. Be as creative as you like. Glue on torn strips of pretty wrapping paper or wallpaper, or cut out pictures from magazines and do découpage, or stick on photocopies of photographs to really personalise the egg, or paint it and stick plastic jewels all over it, or cover it in glitter and tie with a ribbon. Or just go very simple and create golden eggs – simply sprayed or painted with gold paint. Hang again to dry. Once everything is dry, remove the balloon by pricking a hole next to the knot, so that it deflates. Use scissors to cut the egg shape into halves. Put tissue paper inside and fill with treats – sweets or toys. Hold the eggshell together with ribbon or a strip of fabric. Eggceedingly good!

A good gift choice for adults is a stash of those little candy-coated chocolate eggs in a large glass jar tied with a pretty ribbon. An egg hunt is obviously vital if you have little ones – just buy loads of small foil-wrapped eggs and get up early to hide them.

Simple ways to decorate the table

Lay a piece of linen over the table and run a length of lace down the centre. Dot tea lights and single flowers in glass jars along the lace. Tie napkins with lace. Hang out the bunting. And don't forget the cake trick for pudding. Dot butterfly cut-outs over the cake, sprinkle over with glitter dust, remove the templates and sigh with satisfaction – suuuuuper pretty.

Christmas
TIME

AN ADVENT CALENDAR TO LAST FOREVER

(See page 178) I made this because I wanted to recreate the excitement of the Christmas countdown from my own childhood, when we had something similar – its annual appearance a comforting tradition that heralded Christmas. This is my version, which I love because of its simplicity and the fact that each square is big enough to hold a treat for every child in the house, including extras who might have stayed over. It does take some time to make (although it is very easy), but once it's done it's done, and you'll get to bring it out every year, with nothing more arduous to do than fill the pockets.

All you need is red and white felt. Cut out 48 red felt squares measuring 11 x 11cm. Cut out numbers 1 to 24 in white felt. I made my numbers by writing them freestyle on paper, but you could type out the numbers on the computer, playing around with font and size until you find something you like, then use that as a template. Either way you need to cut around the templates, pin to the white felt and cut around. Pin the numbers onto 24 of the red squares and sew on, either by hand or with a machine. (Obviously this is a more arduous task if you don't have a machine – if you do, it won't take long at all.) Just sew a simple line through the centre of each stroke of the letter with white thread. Next place each numbered square on top of a blank one and sew together with red thread, leaving the top open! Again a simple straight stitch around the three sides is the easiest way to do this, although you could use a blanket stitch if sewing by hand. Now all you need is a long string and pegs to hang up the pockets, and a stash of treats to fill.

HOME-MADE STOCKINGS

I know you can easily use pillowcases as 'stockings', but making a special one for each child isn't hard, and it is something they will have forever.

Even in adulthood, don't we still like to wake up to one? The best way to make a template is to get a large piece of paper – a double spread of newspaper is perfect – and draw roughly around the biggest boot you can find. Once you are happy with the shape, cut out your template. Pin it onto the fabric and cut around. You will obviously need two cut-outs to sew together. If the fabric has a pattern, turn the template over for the second, so that they are a mirror image of each other. Felt is great to use for stockings because it doesn't fray. If you are using any other fabric, try to use the selvedge for the top of the stocking so that you don't need to worry about hemming. If you can't, fold the top edge over twice and machine stitch a hem.

Next, decorate the front as you like. You can sew on an initial, or the child's full name (make a template using a font you like on the computer, scale to size and print). Or cut out stars, or shapes, or sew on bells or other Christmas decorations or sequins and beads. Keep it as simple or make it as fancy, as you like. When the front is finished, if you are using felt, stitch the front and back together with a simple blanket stitch in a contrasting tapestry cotton, for a pleasingly home-made look. Otherwise, put the front and back together inside out and machine stitch around, then turn the right way around. Another lovely Christmas tradition that will take you no effort year on year – except for having to fill it of course!

When an envelope is emptied, take it down so the children can clearly see how much closer they're getting to the big day!

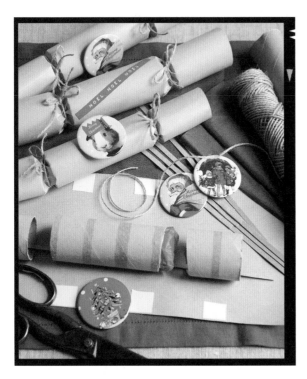

MAKE THE GREATEST
CHRISTMAS CRACKERS EVER

A perfect coming together of the elements of home-making I love best – simple to do plus cheaper and infinitely nicer than anything you can buy. Lovely!

YOU WILL NEED:
- **Cardboard centres of kitchen or loo rolls**
- **Paper to cover**
- **Cracker snaps (buy online, dirt cheap)**
- **Double-sided tape**
- **Whatever you want to put inside**

So here's how you make them. I prefer to use kitchen rolls because they have a bigger circumference, but loo rolls are fine. You need three separate pieces for each cracker – one longer for the middle and two shorter for the ends. If you're using a kitchen roll tube, cut it into three lengths measuring approximately 10cm, 7cm and 7cm. If you're using loo rolls, you'll need a whole one plus another cut in two for the three pieces. Cut a piece of paper (I use parcel paper, but any paper – even newspaper – would work depending on the look you want) about 20 x 35cm. Fix the rolls onto the paper, spaced about 2cm apart, using double-sided tape – you only need a little bit on each.

Now put a snap plus whatever else you like in the centre – it's easiest to fill before the paper is wrapped around completely. Here are just a few suggestions:

- **A game of 'Who Am I?'** Put a sticker in each cracker with the name of a person or animal written on it. Stick it on the forehead of the person to your left and then they have to work out who or what they are during the course of the meal.

- **A game of 'Wink Murder'.** Put a slip of paper in each cracker, all but one showing an image of an eye – the last has a gun. Whoever gets the gun is the murderer and needs to kill people around the table by surreptitiously winking at them. When someone is killed they must feign a dramatic death and are out of the game. Each person is only allowed to make one guess as to who the killer is. The winner is whoever gets it right, or the killer if no one does.

- **A hand-written joke or amazing fact.**
- **Lottery tickets or small gift for adults.**
- **A little toy or stickers for children.**

It's a good idea to wrap the goodies together in a little package of tissue paper so nothing falls out of the ends of the cracker. Roll the paper around and stick together where it overlaps using double-sided tape. Again only a little bit on each roll, as the paper needs to be free to scrunch together between the gaps. Tie ribbon or string between the rolls to secure. Decorate or leave plain, as you want.

Make your own Christmas cards

Making your own cards is actually incredibly simple and cheaper than buying shop-bought ones – and they really are so much better because they are personal. Unleash your creativity and have fun!

If you're going for a photo option, you will need a printer, of course. Edit your photograph if necessary. Turning it black and white can elevate a bog-standard snap to something smarter. Put A4 art card up to 175gsm into your printer – heavier weight card won't go through. Rotate the image so that it is upside down and set it to print at 15 x 10cm size. It has to print upside down or the image will be the wrong way once you've folded the card.

If you have stampers, you could print a festive message inside. Of course, it doesn't have to be a family photograph, or even a photograph at all – a child's drawing can easily be scanned into the computer. Or you could cut out a festive shape like a star or a tree from funky wallpaper. You could print a message on the front with stampers, or use a simple festive stamp on the front. I promise you will never want to go for shop-bought Christmas cards again.

Make salt dough
CHRISTMAS DECORATIONS

A lovely thing to do with the children, and these will look fabulous on the tree.

YOU WILL NEED:
- 2 cups plain flour
- 1 cup table salt
- 1 cup water
- 2 tablespoons lemon juice

Mix together the ingredients to make a dough that will roll out easily. If it's too sticky, add some extra flour. Roll to a thickness of about 3mm and then use cookie cutters to make your shapes. Use a straw or pencil to make holes for the hanging string. Put on trays lined with non-stick baking paper and cook in the oven for about three hours at 100°C. They need to cook low and slow. Or just leave out to air-dry for a couple of days.

Once they're hard (and cool if they've been cooked), you can decorate them. If you want everything to fit a theme, give the children pots of the colour you want and let them splodge it on. If you're feeling more free-spirited, let them go crazy with colour, sequins, sparkles and creativity! These will keep forever, so once the festivities are over, wrap them up in a paper bag and store for next year.

BAKE COOKIES FOR THE CHRISTMAS TREE

It is lovely to combine real edible cookies with the salt dough versions. It looks very pretty, and the children can still snaffle treats from the tree – secretly, or with your blessing! This is an infallible cookie mix, perfect for the job in hand. The dough is very elastic, which makes it easy to work with, and once baked the cookies are hard and robust for the tree, but they still taste really good.

YOU WILL NEED:

- 200g unsalted butter
- 200g caster sugar
- 1 egg
- 400g plain flour
- 2 teaspoons ground cinnamon
- 2 teaspoons ground nutmeg
- pinch of salt

It is quickest and easiest to make these using an electric mixer, with the paddle attachment. Put the sugar in the bowl then add the butter. If the butter is still hard, use your hands to break it up into little pieces as you go, so that it mixes easily. Cream the two together. Beat the egg, then add it to your bowl with the cinnamon, nutmeg and salt and mix. Add the flour. Fold it into the mix before turning the machine back on – use a low speed or a cloud of flour will explode everywhere! The dough is ready when it's formed itself into a ball and doesn't stick to the bowl anymore. If that just isn't happening, add a little more flour – but you shouldn't need to. Once your dough is made, wrap it in clingfilm and stick it in the fridge for at least half an hour. This chills the dough, which means the cookies will keep their shape and won't spread during cooking.

When you're ready to make the cookies, pre-heat the oven to 180°C and cut the dough into three pieces – it's easiest to work with smaller amounts. Sprinkle flour on your work surface and over the rolling pin and roll out the dough so that it is about 2mm thick – obviously it does not need to be exact or even – we are talking tree decorations! Use cutters to stamp out your shapes and put them on a baking tray lined with non-stick baking paper. As these will not spread during cooking, you can lay them out close to each other, so that you can get as many as possible on the tray. You should fill two trays with about 35 cookies altogether. Don't forget to punch a hole through each cookie for hanging string. The cookies need about ten minutes in the oven. They're ready when they start to turn golden brown and slide away from the paper easily. Leave to cool.

Decorate with icing, made of 200g icing sugar mixed with 2 tablespoons of warm water to form a smooth but not too runny paste, and silver balls. If you want to pipe the icing, put it in a plastic bag and cut a small hole in one of the bottom corners.

The smell of cinnamon wafting in the air as these bake signals Christmas is on the way!

DECORATE THE HOUSE

- Mini conifers dotted around the house ooze low-key festive style. You can buy them very cheaply from a garden centre. Just repot in basic terracotta pots or tie a piece of fabric around the plastic pots. (Line it with a bit of bin liner first so it doesn't leak when you water it.)
- Red ribbons tied to door handles add a splash of colour.
- A wonderful way to make the house look stylish for free is to use little off-cuts from tree branches that get snipped off by garden centers – you should be able to pick up a bag of pieces for nothing. Run a string of fairy lights along a shelf, mantelpiece, or down the centre of the table on Christmas Day and piece together the off-cuts over and around the lights. Holly and ivy or pinecones look great too. Bling-free style.
- Tea lights look absolutely beautiful suspended from a branch, either left natural or sprayed white, and hung over the table.
- Tie a cascade of ribbons to a hanging light. This is such an effective way of giving festive grotto-style chic to an entrance hall. Add a ball of mistletoe too, as long as you've not got pets or very little ones, and don't need to worry about its poisonous berries being consumed if they drop onto the floor.

DECORATE YOUR FRONT DOOR

Having been scarred by the theft of a beautiful (and expensive) wreath from my front door, I came up with a low-budget version to make the door look festive and stylish, without worrying that some toe-rag will come along and swipe it. Obviously if you live somewhere where no such concerns affect you, feel free to buy a lavish wreath, or festoon my version with berries, baubles, bells – whatever grabs your fancy. Anyway here's the basic version, created out of necessity, but which I actually love more than my old upmarket one, for its simplicity and value. It couldn't be simpler – it's just a branch of a Christmas tree. If you're lucky you can pick one up for free in the garden centre or market, or pay a token amount. Tie on a ribbon and it looks pretty festive. They look great on doors inside the house too, dressed up with bells.

The Christmas
COUNTDOWN

Just tick the boxes as you go, and before you know it, it will be Christmas Eve and you'll feel as relaxed as a cat in the sunshine – ooh yeah!

⭐ 1 SEPTEMBER

BOOK THE FRONT ROW FOR THE HOT TICKET HOLIDAY SHOW It is super early, but if you want to see any show or ballet in the week running up to Christmas you need to be one of the first in line for tickets. And anyway it takes no effort at all to sit at your computer and book online. Roll on Christmas, when you'll have the best seats in the house!

⭐ 15 OCTOBER

BOOK FATHER CHRISTMAS If you've got little ones, going to see Father Christmas in a big department store is one of those great festive traditions, but if you don't want to end up having to see him in early November, a little bit of forward planning is needed. Basically you need to book as soon as your chosen venue opens its booking because tickets go extraordinarily quickly – they are free after all (or only cost a nominal amount), and give you one of the biggest Christmas-time bangs for your buck. Put in the call or check online today, because this is when booking opens for most major department stores.

⭐ 25 OCTOBER

START A CHRISTMAS PRESENT NOTEBOOK It's great being organised by starting Christmas shopping early. The only hazard is, it's easy to forget what you've bought until you get everything out to wrap and suddenly realise quite how much has been stashed away. Keeping a Christmas notebook is a simple way of staying on track. Firstly, write down the names of who you've got to get presents for and gift ideas for them. When you've bought or made something, write it in and tick that person off. On Christmas Day use the book to write down presents received, so that you don't forget who to thank and what for. Also, this way you'll have a clear record of everything given and received, which will come in handy next year when you're coming up with ideas and can't remember if you're repeating yourself. Why not get in touch with friends and family now to set a limit on how much everyone spends on each other, so that things don't get out of hand. And remember, don't overbuy for the kids. By the time presents from friends and family have piled under the tree alongside yours, it can get ridiculous, and you'll regret it on Christmas Day as the children carelessly toss aside opened presents, greedy for the next one.

⭐ 1 NOVEMBER

START HORDING KITCHEN AND TOILET ROLL CENTRES for making your own crackers. I know, it sounds like an extra hassle you don't need, but these are so worth doing, and are really easy (see page 180). If you build them little by little, they take barely any effort to make, and I promise you will have much more fun with crackers you've designed to entertain your guests, rather than shop-bought ones that are forgotten as soon as they're pulled.

⭐ 12 November

ORDER CRACKER SNAPS Just type the two words into your search engine and numerous sellers will pop up online. Buy the 33cm length – you can always cut them down a little if necessary to fit your cracker, but if you get snaps that are too short, you'll be stuck.

⭐ 13 November

PRINT OUT CRACKER JOKES There are gazillions of jokes floating about on the web, just spend a little time today finding some funny ones for your home-made Christmas crackers. Copy and paste onto a page and print ready to cut into rib-tickling strips for the crackers. An alternative is to opt for amazing facts – which again you can find a plethora of online.

⭐ 15 November

BUY THE STOCKING FILLERS Get them out of the way now, and you can forget all about them until Christmas Eve. The good thing about sorting them early is that you can buy stuff online with no worries about it shipping in time. When the parcels arrive, wrap everything in colour-coded tissue paper for each child, hide it all away in a pillow case, and come Christmas Eve, you know which packages go in which stocking. Easy.

⭐ 17 November

SORT PRINTED ADDRESS LABELS FOR ENVELOPES A little time spent on this now will save you so much more later. Also, it means you'll know how many cards you need to buy or make.If you are lucky, your computer will have a programme for making labels. If not, search online for a template. It's a good idea to put all the addresses you use regularly on one or two pages, so that you can easily reprint throughout the year for birthday thank yous etc.

⭐ 18 November

STOCK UP ON BATTERIES Now is a good time to stock up on batteries to avoid the Christmas Day 'batteries not included' nightmare.

⭐ 1 December

ORDER THE MEAT Even if you always buy your meat from the supermarket, I would recommend this as the one time of year to order from the butcher. Knowing you've got the meat sorted early makes shopping for the holiday so much easier because you won't have a last-minute panic about whether the supermarket will have a turkey or goose big enough to feed everyone. Also, the butcher will advise on the size of bird and other quantities you need, which eliminates the guesswork and worrying that you might not have got it right. So make your list and give it to the butcher today. Don't forget all the trimmings plus something to slow roast for Christmas Eve, and a gammon for light meals over the holiday. Now you can forget about the meat until Christmas. Hooray!

⭐ 2 December

MAKE YOUR OWN CHRISTMAS CARDS Sending Christmas cards can be a rather soulless box-ticking exercise. Think about what you like to receive. Does opening a shop-bought card with a basic 'Dear blah, Happy Christmas love from blah' make you feel glad to have received it, or connected to the sender? But then you open a card that someone has spent time thinking about. Maybe it's a photograph, a child's drawing or a thoughtful message inside. Those are the cards that are lovely to receive, so make sure that's what you send. Cards are very easy and pleasing to make (see page 181) but if you really don't have the time or inclination to make your own, at least write a thoughtful and personal message inside.

★ **3 December**

WRAP PRESENTS AS YOU BUY THEM to avoid a last-minute frenzy. The large quantities of wrapping paper you need at Christmas can be so expensive, unless you go for the really cheap stuff, which is then a nightmare to use because it tears so easily. Check out home-made wrapping paper (see page 151) for how to make your own fabulous paper very cheaply.

★ **4 December**

HAVE A PRE–CHRISTMAS CLEAR-OUT The run-up to Christmas is the perfect time to go through kids' toys and decide what can go to clear space for the pending influx of new treasures. Beware, the minute the children spot something heading out the door to the charity shop is the moment when they'll suddenly decide the game/doll they haven't thought about for months is their favourite thing and you simply can't get rid of it. You need to be tough, or do it while they're at school!

★ **7 December**

PUT UP THE TREE AND DECORATE THE HOUSE Use the weekend that falls closest to the 7th to choose a tree with the children and decorate it together. Check out some simple, stylish ideas about what to make and how to decorate (see page 183).

★ **8 December**

IF YOU DON'T HAVE ONE, BUY A BASTER These are absolutely essential if you are going to cook a goose because of the amount of molten fat you will need to remove from the pan during cooking. It saves you from having to remove the goose from the oven and wrestle with it each time you want to pour off the fat – instead you can just suction it out with no sweat.

★ **9 December**

SORT THE TEACHER'S GIFTS Why not make some caramelised nuts or truffles (see page 146), or plant some bulbs in a basket. Don't forget the caretaker, who probably has one of the most thankless tasks in school.

★ **12 December**

ARRANGE FOR FATHER CHRISTMAS TO CALL ON CHRISTMAS EVE My dad always calls the girls on Christmas Eve, in the guise of Father Christmas – if he's with us, he has to hide in another room to make the call – and they absolutely love it. Even my eldest is prepared to suspend disbelief as she relishes the possibility that she might really be talking to the big man himself! Here's a great way to make the call look even more authentic – edit the contact details of whoever's making the call so when the call comes through it flashes up on the screen saying 'Father Christmas calling...' with a picture of him to match. It's brilliant! Don't forget to change back though or you'll be rumbled later!

★ **15 December**

MAKE THE CRACKERS See page 180.

★ **18 December**

THE FOOD AND DRINK SHOP Make a good list before you go and get all the non-perishables and anything that can freeze sorted now.

★ **19 December**

TIP THE BIN MEN AND POSTMAN And the milkman too if you have one. A small token of appreciation for some of the people we rely on, but rarely see.

⭐ 22 December

PICK UP YOUR MEAT FROM THE BUTCHER Picking it up today is good for several reasons. First, you avoid the nightmare queues that start to sprout from the 23rd. Second, it gives you plenty of time to prepare the meat so it is oven-ready and will require no effort beyond bunging it in the oven on Christmas Day. Prepare the goose or the turkey and put it in the roasting tin, ready to go. Wrap the bacon around the chipolatas and place on a tray ready for the oven. Cover both with clingfilm. Think ready meals – you're just doing the assembly work yourself. Getting all of the preparation done now makes timing the meal on Christmas Day a cinch.

⭐ 23 December

THE FINAL FOOD SHOP The meat's sorted, the freezer's full, the drink's been bought – this final shop should be a breeze. Just remember, you're not hunkering down for months – it's only a few days! No need to go overboard!

⭐ 24 December

LAY THE TABLE READY FOR CHRISTMAS DAY BEFORE YOU GO TO BED It's a really good idea to get this time-consuming job out of the way the day before, so you've got some time to think about prettifying the table, rather than throwing it all together in a window between present-opening and cooking, as you panic about whether you've got enough clean plates and cutlery to put out. Don't stress if anything gets spilled on the tablecloth at breakfast. If you're that bothered, cover any messes with a strategically placed bowl of cranberry sauce or a candle. You definitely don't want to find yourself with two tablecloths to wash when it's all over.

> ★ **Wonder Tip**
>
> As long as it's very cold outside, use your car boot as a spare fridge over the holiday period. It will easily store your meat and any other supplies that won't fit into the fridge. Genius!

⭐ 25 December

REMEMBER TO HAVE FUN Hopefully, having got here in baby steps, you'll be breezy, chilled and ready for a great day. Don't spoil it all now by going into overdrive trying to do everything yourself. Get everyone to pitch in: vegetable peeling – a perfect job for kids; slicing – dad can do that; making the gravy – mum, etc, etc. It's about everyone being together, having fun – not you being slave for the day. Just don't forget to make sure the champagne's in the fridge, so you can enjoy a nice chilled glass or two – you deserve it!

Above all, don't overcomplicate. Christmas is about traditions, togetherness and having fun. Keep it simple and enjoy!

A FINAL THOUGHT. How you spend your time defines you. If you spend it all slogging away trying to keep a perfect home, you'll only feel stressed, tired and under-appreciated. No husband or kids ever marvel at how perfectly pristine the house is, or appreciate it. Sure, they complain when they can't find something, or there's no food in the fridge. Let them. That's how they appreciate how much you do actually do, to keep their lives running smoothly. For your own sanity, you don't want to preside over chaos, but equally, for your own sanity, you have to realise when something's gotta give. Keeping a well-organised home is actually the key to saving time that you can spend doing stuff that keeps you sane. And when you come across something that works, remember to pass it on. Life's so much better when we help each other out.

INDEX

THANK YOU

As with any book, turning my private pet project into this has entailed the support, help, hardwork and talent of many people, to whom I am incredibly grateful.

The team at Kyle Books have been amazing and I feel very fortunate to have got to know them and to have worked with them on this: Catharine (my brilliant, calm, talented editor), Judith, Julia, Victoria and Kyle, of course, who each played a vital part in helping to shape the finished item. I am eternally grateful to Zeb, who put me in touch with Kyle in the first place and for her faith and support from the outset.

One team of wonderwomen created another, when they pulled together Rachel, Rita, Victoria and Laura to do the book photography, styling and design. Together they have helped to create something that surpassed my expectations.

Writing a book was a new departure for me, and I am very thankful to have had extra special agent Felicity to hold my hand and help me navigate this exciting new world.

I also need to thank my fabulous butcher, John Stenton, and Kiran Sisi (as well as his Dad, Howard) from my brilliant local hardware store, for agreeing to be photographed for the book. Over the years they have given me so much advice and many tips – I feel extremely lucky to have them just around the corner.

And of course, through everything, my mum and dad, family and friends are a vital support and source of love, laughter, encouragement and inspiration I couldn't do without. So much of what I am trying to do with this book and with my own family is to recreate the happy childhood I was lucky enough to have, so I need to say a special thank you to Mum and Dad for that.

Which brings me to my husband and our girls – who are all of the above and more. This is a book about how you spend your time, and I know that through the course of writing it, I have sometimes had to let things slide more than I should at home to get this done. Thank you Craig, Maya, Iona and Honor. You complete me.

Joanna